Praxis
0049
5049

Middle School English Language Arts

Teacher Certification Exam

By: Sharon Wynne, M.S.

XAMonline, INC.
Boston

XAMonline, Inc.
25 First Street, Suite 106
Cambridge, MA 02141
Toll Free 1-800-301-4647
Email: info@xamonline.com
Web: www.xamonline.com
Fax: 1-617-583-5552

Library of Congress Cataloging-in-Publication Data

Wynne, Sharon A.
    Middle School English Language Arts 0049, 5049: Teacher Certification / Sharon A. Wynne. -4th ed.
    ISBN 978-1-60787-345-7
    1. Middle School English Language Arts 0049, 5049.   2. Study Guides.   3. Praxis
    4. Teachers' Certification & Licensure.   5. Careers

Disclaimer:
The opinions expressed in this publication are the sole works of XAMonline and were created independently from the National Education Association, Educational Testing Service, or any State Department of Education, National Evaluation Systems or other testing affiliates.

Between the time of publication and printing, state specific standards as well as testing formats and website information may change that is not included in part or in whole within this product. Sample test questions are developed by XAMonline and reflect similar content as on real tests; however, they are not former tests. XAMonline assembles content that aligns with state standards but makes no claims nor guarantees teacher candidates a passing score. Numerical scores are determined by testing companies such as NES or ETS and then are compared with individual state standards. A passing score varies from state to state.

Printed in the United States of America   œ-1

Praxis Middle School English Language Arts 0049, 5049
ISBN: 978-1-60787-345-7

TABLE OF CONTENTS

Great Study and Testing Tips!

What to study in order to prepare for the subject assessments is the focus of this study guide but equally important is *how* you study.

You can increase your chances of truly mastering the information by taking some simple, but effective steps.

Study Tips:

1. <u>Some foods aid the learning process</u>. Foods such as milk, nuts, seeds, rice, and oats help study efforts by releasing natural memory enhancers called CCKs (*cholecystokinin*) composed of *tryptopha*n, *choline*, and *phenylalanine*. These chemicals enhance the neurotransmitters associated with memory. Before studying, try a light, protein-rich meal of eggs, turkey, and fish. These foods release the memory enhancing chemicals. The better the connections, the more you comprehend.

Likewise, before you take a test, stick to a light snack of energy boosting and relaxing foods. A glass of milk, a piece of fruit, or some peanuts will release various memory-boosting chemicals and help you relax and focus on the subject at hand.

2. <u>Learn to take great notes</u>. If your notes are scrawled all over the paper, it fragments the flow of the information. Your notes can be much clearer through use of proper formatting. A very effective format is called the *"Cornell Method."* Here's how it's done:

> Take a sheet of loose-leaf lined notebook paper and draw a line all the way down the paper about 1-2" from the left-hand edge.

> Draw another line across the width of the paper about 1–2" up from the bottom. Repeat this process on the reverse side of the page.

Look at the result. You have ample room for notes, a left hand margin for special emphasis items or inserting supplementary data from the textbook, a large area at the bottom for a brief summary, and a little rectangular space for just about anything you want.

3. <u>Get the concept then the details</u>. Too often we focus on the details without understanding of the concept. However, if you simply memorize only dates, places, or names, you may well miss the whole point of the subject.

A key way to understand information and concepts is to put what you've learned into your own words. If you are working from a textbook, automatically summarize each paragraph in your mind. If you are outlining a text, *rephrase* the material in your own words.

You will remember your own thoughts and words better and subconsciously associate the important details to the core concepts.

4. <u>Ask *Why?*</u> Break down written material paragraph by paragraph and don't forget the captions under the illustrations. Also, ask *why* when reading information. For example: If the heading is "Stream Erosion", flip it around to read "Why do streams erode?" Then answer the questions.

If you train your mind to think in a series of questions and answers, not only will you learn more, but it also helps to lessen the test anxiety because you are used to answering questions.

5. <u>Read for reinforcement and future needs</u>. Even if you only have 10 minutes, put your notes or a book in your hand. Your mind is similar to a computer; you have to input data in order to have it processed. *By reading, you are creating the neural connections for future retrieval.* The more times you read something, the more you reinforce the learning of ideas.

Even if you don't fully understand something on the first pass, *your mind stores much of the material for later recall.*

6. <u>Relax to learn so go into exile</u>. Our bodies respond to an inner clock called biorhythms. Burning the midnight oil works well for some people but not for everyone.

If possible, set aside a particular place to study that is free of distractions. Shut off the television, cell phone, and pager and exile your friends and family.

If you really are bothered by silence, try background music. Light classical music at a low volume has been shown to aid in concentration. Music that evokes pleasant emotions without lyrics is highly suggested. Try just about anything by Mozart.

7. <u>Use arrows not highlighters</u>. At best, it's difficult to read a page full of yellow, pink, blue, and green streaks. Try staring at a neon sign for a while and you'll soon see that the colors obscure the message.

A quick note, a brief dash of color, an underline, or an arrow pointing to a particular passage is much clearer than many highlighted words.

8. <u>Change your location</u>. Psychologists have found that changing your study location every so often can help you retain information more effectively. So, move to a new location every 20 minutes or so.

9. <u>Budget your study time</u>. Although you shouldn't ignore any of the material, *allocate your available study time in the same ratio that topics may appear on the test.*

Testing Tips:

1. <u>Get smart, play dumb</u>. Don't read anything into the question. Don't make an assumption that the test writer is looking for something else than what is asked. Stick to the question as written.

2. <u>Read the question and all the choices *twice* before answering the question</u>. Read and reread both the question and the answers.

If you don't have a clue as to the right answer, leave it blank. Go on to the other questions, as they may provide a clue as to how to answer the skipped questions.

If later on you still can't answer the skipped questions . . . *Guess.* There is no penalty for guessing.

3. <u>Turn the question into a statement</u>. Look at the way the questions are worded. The syntax of the question usually provides a clue. Does it seem more familiar as a statement rather than as a question? Does it sound strange?

By turning a question into a statement, you may be able to spot if an answer sounds right, and it may trigger recognition.

4. <u>Look for hidden clues</u>. It's actually very difficult to compose multiple-foil (choice) questions without giving away part of the answer in the options presented.

In most multiple-choice questions, you can often readily eliminate one or two of the potential answers. In doing so, your odds of choosing the correct answer have greatly improved.

5. <u>Trust your instincts</u>. For every fact that you have read, you subconsciously retain something of that knowledge. If you are uncertain about an answer, go with your basic instincts. **Your first impression on how to answer a question is often correct.**

6. <u>Watch the clock</u>! You have a set amount of time to answer the questions. Don't get bogged down trying to answer a single question at the expense of 10 questions that you can quickly answer.

COMPETENCY 1.0 READING AND LITERATURE

Skill 1.1   Identifying major works and authors of literature appropriate for adolescents

Prior to twentieth century research on child development and literature's relationship to that development, books for adolescents were primarily didactic. They taught subjects such as history, manners, and morals. Over the years literature for young people has changed dramatically in both quantity and depth. Below is a short history.

MIDDLE AGES

As early as the eleventh century, Anselm, the Archbishop of Canterbury, wrote an encyclopedia designed to instill in children the beliefs and principles of conduct acceptable in medieval society. Early monastic translations of the Bible and other religious writings, written in Latin, were meant for the edification of the upper class.

One early text was the *hornbook*. The fifteenth-century hornbooks were designed to teach reading and religious lessons. Additionally, William Caxton printed English versions of *Aesop's Fables*, Malory's *Le Morte d'Arthur* and stories from Greek and Roman mythology. Though printed for adults, tales of the adventures of Odysseus and the Arthurian knights were also popular with literate adolescents.

RENAISSANCE

The Renaissance saw the introduction of the inexpensive chapbooks, small in size and sixteen to sixty-four pages in length. **Chapbooks** were condensed versions of myths and fairy tales. Designed for the common people, chapbooks were imperfect grammatically but were immensely popular because of their adventurous content. Though most of the serious, educated adults frowned on the sometimes-vulgar little books, they received praise from Richard Steele of *Tatler* fame for inspiring his grandson's interest in reading.

Meanwhile, the Puritans' three most popular reads were the Bible, John Foxe's *Book of Martyrs*, and John Bunyan's *Pilgrim's Progress*. Though venerating religious martyrs and preaching the moral propriety that was to lead to eternal happiness, the stories of the *Book of Martyrs* were often lurid in their descriptions of the fate of the damned. Not written for children and difficult reading even for adults, *Pilgrim's Progress* was as attractive to adolescents for its adventurous plot as for its moral outcome.

In Puritan America, the *New England Primer* set forth the prayers, catechisms, Bible verses, and illustrations meant to instruct children in the Puritan ethic. The seventeenth-century French used fables and fairy tales to entertain adults but children found them enjoyable as well.

SEVENTEENTH CENTURY

Literature specifically written for young people first appeared in the late seventeenth century. Pierre Perrault's *Fairy Tales*, Jean de la Fontaine's retellings of famous fables, Mme. d'Aulnoy's novels based on old folktales, and Mme. de Beaumont's *Beauty and the Beast* were written to delight as well as to instruct young people. In England, publisher John Newbury was the first to publish a line of books for children. These included a translation of Perrault's *Tales of Mother Goose; A Little Pretty Pocket-Book*, which was "intended for instruction and amusement" but decidedly moralistic and bland in comparison to the previous century's chapbooks; and *The Renowned History of Little Goody Two Shoes*, allegedly written by Oliver Goldsmith for a juvenile audience.

EIGHTEENTH CENTURY

However, into the eighteenth century most adolescents were finding their reading pleasure in adult books: Daniel Defoe's *Robinson Crusoe*, Jonathan Swift's *Gulliver's Travels*, and Johann Wyss's *Swiss Family Robinson*. More books were being written for children, but the moral didacticism, though less religious, was always present. The short stories of Maria Edgeworth, the four-volume *The History of Sandford and Merton* by Thomas Day, and Martha Farquharson's twenty-six-volume *Elsie Dinsmore* series dealt with pious protagonists who learned restraint, repentance, and rehabilitation from sin.

Two bright spots in this period of didacticism were Jean Jacques Rousseau's *Emile* and Charles and Mary Lamb's simplified versions of Shakespeare's plays, *The Tales of Shakespeare*. Rousseau believed that a child's abilities were enhanced by a free, happy life and the Lambs subscribed to the notion that children were entitled to entertaining literature in language comprehensible to them.

NINETEENTH CENTURY

Child/adolescent literature truly began its rise in nineteenth-century Europe. Hans Christian Andersen's *Fairy Tales* were fanciful adaptations of the somber revisions of the Grimm brothers in the previous century. Andrew Lang's series of colorful fairy books contain the folklores of many nations and are still part of the collections of many modern libraries. Clement Moore's "A Visit from St. Nicholas" is a cheery, non-threatening child's view of the "Night before Christmas." The humor of Lewis Carroll's books about Alice's adventures, Edward Lear's poems with caricatures, and Lucretia Nole's stories of the Philadelphia Peterkin family, were all full of fancy and not a smidgen of morality.

Other popular Victorian novels introduced the modern fantasy and science fiction genres: William Makepeace Thackeray's *The Rose and the Ring*, Charles Dickens' *The Magic Fishbone*, and Jules Verne's *Twenty Thousand Leagues Under the Sea*. Adventure to exotic places became a popular topic: Rudyard Kipling's *Jungle Book*, Verne's *Around the World in Eighty Days*, and Robert Louis Stevenson's *Treasure Island* and *Kidnapped*. In 1884 the first English translation Johanna Spyre's *Heidi* appeared.

North America was also finding its voice for adolescent readers. American Louisa May Alcott's *Little Women* and Canadian L.M. Montgomery's *Anne of Green Gables* ushered in the modern age of realistic fiction. American youth were enjoying the adventures of Tom Sawyer and Huckleberry Finn. For the first time children were able to read books about real people just like themselves.

TWENTIETH CENTURY

The literature of the twentieth century is extensive and diverse, and, as in previous centuries, much influenced by the adults who write, edit, and select books for youth consumption. In the first third of the century, suitable adolescent literature dealt with children from good homes with large families. These books projected an image of a peaceful, rural existence. Though the characters and plots were realistic, the stories maintained focus on topics that were considered emotionally and intellectually proper. Popular at this time were Laura Ingalls Wilder's *Little House on the Prairie* series and Carl Sandburg's biography *Abe Lincoln Grows Up*. English author J.R.R. Tolkein's fantasy *The Hobbit* paved the way for modern adolescent readers' fascination with the works of Piers Antony, Madelaine L'Engle, and Anne McCaffery.

TODAY'S LITERATURE FOR ADOLESCENTS AND YOUNG ADULTS

For Sixth Grade

The following list of classic and contemporary works combines elements of multiple theories. Functioning at the concrete operations stage (Piaget), being of the "good person" orientation (Kohlberg), still highly dependent on external rewards (Bandura), and exhibiting all five needs previously discussed from Maslow's hierarchy, eleven- to twelve-year olds should appreciate the following titles, which are grouped by reading level. These titles are also chosen for interest at that grade level and do not reflect high-interest titles for older readers who do not read at grade level. Some high-interest titles will be cited later.

Reading level 6.0 to 6.9

- Barrett, William. *Lilies of the Field*
- Cormier, Robert. *Other Bells for Us to Ring*
- Dahl, Roald. *Danny, Champion of the World; Charlie and the Chocolate Factory*
- Lindgren, Astrid. *Pippi Longstocking*
- Lindbergh, Anne. *Three Lives to Live*
- Lowry, Lois. *Rabble Starkey*
- Naylor, Phyllis. *The Year of the Gopher; Reluctantly Alice*
- Peck, Robert Newton. *Arly*
- Speare, Elizabeth. *The Witch of Blackbird Pond*
- Sleator, William. *The Boy Who Reversed Himself*

For Seventh and Eighth Grades

Most seventh- and eighth-grade students, according to learning theory, are still functioning cognitively, psychologically, and morally as sixth graders. As these are not inflexible standards, there are some twelve- and thirteen-year olds who are much more mature socially, intellectually, and physically than the younger children who share the same school. They are becoming concerned with establishing individual and peer group identities that present conflicts with breaking from authority and the rigidity of rules.

Some students at this age are still tied firmly to the family and its expectations while others identify more with those their own age or older. Enrichment reading for this group must help the students cope with life's rapid changes or provide escape and thus must be either realistic or fantastic depending on the child's needs. Adventures and mysteries (the *Hardy Boys* and *Nancy Drew* series) are still popular today. Today preteens are also becoming more interested in biographies of contemporary figures rather than legendary figures of the past.

Reading level 7.0 to 7.9

- Armstrong, William. *Sounder*
- Bagnold, Enid. *National Velvet*
- Barrie, James. *Peter Pan*
- London, Jack. *White Fang; The Call of the Wild*
- Lowry, Lois. *Taking Care of Terrific*
- McCaffrey, Anne. The *Dragonsinger* series
- Montgomery, L. M. *Anne of Green Gables* and sequels
- Steinbeck, John. *The Pearl*
- Tolkien, J. R. R. *The Hobbit*
- Zindel, Paul. *The Pigman*

Reading level 8.0 to 8.9

- ⊙ Cormier, Robert. *I Am the Cheese*
- ⊙ McCullers, Carson. *The Member of the Wedding*
- ⊙ North, Sterling. *Rascal*
- ⊙ Twain, Mark. *The Adventures of Tom Sawyer*
- ⊙ Zindel, Paul. *My Darling, My Hamburger*

For Ninth Grade

Depending upon the school environment, a ninth grader may be top dog in a junior high school or underdog in a high school. Much of the child's social development and thus his or her reading interests become motivated by peer associations. A ninth grader is technically an adolescent operating at the early stages of formal operations in cognitive development. The perception of identity becomes well defined and the ninth grader is fully aware of the ethics required by society. Readers at this stage are more receptive to the challenges of classic literature but still enjoy popular teen novels.

Reading level 9.0 to 9.9

- ⊙ Defoe, Daniel. *Robinson Crusoe*
- ⊙ Dickens, Charles. *David Copperfield*
- ⊙ Golding, William. *Lord of the Flies*
- ⊙ Greenberg, Joanne. *I Never Promised You a Rose Garden*
- ⊙ Kipling, Rudyard. *Captains Courageous*
- ⊙ Lee, Harper. *To Kill a Mockingbird*
- ⊙ Nordhoff, Charles. *Mutiny on the Bounty*
- ⊙ Shelley, Mary. *Frankenstein*
- ⊙ Washington, Booker T. *Up From Slavery*

For Tenth through Twelfth Grades

All high school sophomores, juniors, and seniors can handle most other literature except for a few of the most difficult titles like *Moby-Dick* or *Vanity Fair*. However, since many high school students do not progress to the eleventh- or twelfth-grade reading level, they will still have their favorites among authors whose writings they can understand. Many will struggle with assigned novels but still read high-interest books for pleasure. A few high-interest titles are listed below without reading-level designations, though most are 6.0 to 7.9.

- ⊙ Bauer, Joan. *Squashed*
- ⊙ Borland, Hal. *When the Legends Die*
- ⊙ Danzinger, Paula. *Remember Me to Herald Square*
- ⊙ Duncan, Lois. *Stranger with my Face*
- ⊙ Hamilton, Virginia. *The Planet of Junior Brown*
- ⊙ Hinton, S. E. *The Outsiders*

⊙ Paterson, Katherine. *The Great Gilly Hopkins*

Teachers of students at all levels must be familiar with the materials offered by libraries in their own schools. Only then can teachers guide students to appropriate selections for their social age and reading-level development.

Today's adolescent literature is extremely diverse. Fiction for the middle group, usually ages ten/eleven to fourteen/fifteen, often deals with issues of coping with internal and external changes. Because authors in the twentieth century have produced larger numbers of realistic fiction titles, adolescents can now find many issues and problems presented openly and honestly in their reading.

Teachers of middle/junior high school students see the greatest change in interests and reading abilities. Fifth and sixth graders, included in elementary grades in many schools, are viewed as older children while seventh and eighth graders are viewed as preadolescent. Ninth graders definitely view themselves as teenagers. Their literature choices will often be governed more by interest than by ability—hence the wealth of high-interest, low readability books that have flooded the market in recent years. Tenth through twelfth graders will still select high-interest books for pleasure reading but are also easily encouraged to stretch their literature muscles by reading more classics.

Because of rapid social changes, topics that once did not interest young people until they reached their teens—such as suicide, gangs, and homosexuality—are now subjects of books for younger readers. The plethora of high-interest books reveals how the market has adapted to that need. These high-interest books are now readable for younger children whose reading levels are at or above normal. No matter how tastefully written, some content is inappropriate for younger readers. The problem becomes not so much steering readers toward books at their reading level but rather steering them toward books with content that is appropriate to their level of cognitive and social development. A fifth-grader may be able to read V.C. Andrews's book *Flowers in the Attic* but not possess the social/moral development to handle the deviant behavior of the characters.

Because of the complex changes affecting adolescents, the teacher must be well versed in learning theory and child development as well as competent to teach the subject matter of language and literature.

Skill 1.2   Interpreting, paraphrasing, and comparing various types of texts, including fiction, poetry, essays, and other nonfiction

INTERPRETING LITERATURE

Good literature is rich in language and concepts. Students should learn how to interpret good literature. Here are some literary devices that students should learn to recognize:

⊙ **Ambiguity**: Ambiguity occurs when meaning cannot be determined by its context. Ambiguity may be introduced accidentally or intentionally. It often confuses readers and disrupts the flow of reading.

⊙ **Connotation**: The connotation is the suggested or emotional implications and associations of a word rather than the word's literal definition.

⊙ **Symbolism**: A symbol is a person, place, or thing that stands for both itself and something beyond itself. In most cases, a symbol stands for something that has a deeper meaning than its literal meaning. Symbols can have personal, cultural, or universal associations. Understanding symbols can help unearth a meaning the author might have intended but not expressed explicitly.

⊙ **Rhythm**: Rhythm refers to the harmony between the words chosen and the smoothness, rapidity, or disjointedness of the way those words are written. Reading text out loud is an easy way to impart understanding of literary rhythm.

⊙ **Rhyme**: Writing with rhyme can be especially effective on reader response. Think about the success Dr. Seuss had with his rhyming style. Rhyme is tricky, however. Used ineffectively or unnecessarily, it can break up the entire rhythm of the piece or fog the reader's understanding. Rhyme should be used only when it is beneficial to the format of the piece.

⊙ **Diction**: Diction is simply the right word in the right spot for the right purpose. The hallmark of a great writer is precise, unique, and memorable diction.

⊙ **Imagery**: Imagery is language that appeals to the five senses. An author might use imagery to give readers a vivid or realistic picture of a scene or character. Imagery can also conjure up a reader's past experiences (the smell of the ocean, the feeling of their childhood blanket) thereby enriching the mental picture.

⊙ **Tone**: Tone is the attitude a writer takes toward his or her subject or literary work. For example, the tone of a piece of writing might be passionate, unemotional, sarcastic, cynical, or solemn. Speakers reveal their tone in their voice. However, writers must use diction and other devices to reveal tone.

⊙ **Theme**: Theme is the central meaning or idea in a literary work.

PARAPHRASING TEXT

Readers must learn to paraphrase what they read. This will help when they are writing an analysis essay or conducting research. Paraphrasing is the art of rewording text and its goal is to maintain the original purpose of the text while translating it into the reader's own words.

Encourage students to concentrate on the meaning, not on the words. Do not change concept words, special terms, or proper names. There are numerous ways to effectively paraphrase:

⊙ Change key words' form or part of speech. Example: "American news **coverage** is frequently **biased** in favor of Western views" becomes "When American journalists **cover** events, they often display a Western **bias**."

⊙ Use synonyms or "relationship words." Look for a relationship word, such as **contrast, cause,** or **effect,** and replace it with a word that conveys a similar meaning, thus creating a different structure for the sentence. Example: "**Unlike** many cats, Purrdy can sit on command" becomes "Most cats are not able to be trained, **but** Purrdy can sit on command."

⊙ Use synonyms of phrases and words. Example: "**the start of the decade**" becomes "**around the early 1950s.**"

⊙ Also try to paraphrase entire paragraphs rather than individual sentences. Think about the information after reading and then write. Tell students not to look at the text when they are paraphrasing.

RESPONDING TO LITERATURE

Reading literature involves a reciprocal interaction between the reader and the text. There are four main types of responses.

1. **Emotional**
   The reader can identify with the characters and situations so as to project himself into the story. The reader feels a sense of satisfaction by associating aspects of his own life with the people, places, and events in the literature. Emotional responses are observed in a reader's verbal and non-verbal reactions; for example, laughter, comments on its effects, and retelling or dramatizing the action.

2. **Interpretive**
   Interpretive responses can result in inferences about character development, setting, or plot or in an analysis of style elements such as metaphor, simile, allusion, rhythm, and tone. Interpretive responses can also result in outcomes derived from the information provided in the narrative and in an assessment of the author's intent.

3. **Critical**
   Critical responses involve making value judgments about the quality of a piece of literature. Reactions to the effectiveness of the writer's style and language use can be observed through discussion and written reactions.

4. **Evaluative**
   Evaluative responses consider such factors as how well the piece of literature represents its genre, how well it reflects the social and ethical mores of society, and how well the author has approached the subject for freshness and slant.

Middle school readers will exhibit both emotional and interpretive responses. Naturally, making interpretive responses depends on the degree of knowledge the student has of literary elements. Being able to say why a particular book was boring or why a particular poem made him sad evidences a child's critical reactions on a fundamental level.

Adolescents in ninth and tenth grades should begin to make critical responses by addressing the *specific* language and genre characteristics of literature. Evaluative responses are more difficult to detect and are rarely made by any but a few advanced high school students. However, if the teacher knows what to listen for, she can recognize evaluative responses and incorporate them into discussions.

For example, if a student says, "I don't understand why that character is doing that," he is making an interpretive response to character motivation. However, if he goes on to say, "What good is that action?" he is giving an evaluative response that should be explored in terms of "What good should it do and why isn't that positive action happening?"

At the emotional level, the student might say, "I almost broke into a sweat when he was describing the heat in the burning house." An interpretive response might be, "The author uses descriptive adjectives to bring his setting to life." Critically, the student adds, "The author's use of descriptive language contributes to the success of the narrative and maintains reader interest through the whole story." If he goes on to wonder why the author allows the grandmother in the story to die in the fire, he is making an evaluative response.

Levels of Response

The levels of reader response will depend largely on the reader's level of social, psychological, and intellectual development. Most middle school students have progressed beyond merely involving themselves in the story enough to be able to retell the events in some logical sequence or to describe the feeling that the story evoked. They are aware to some degree that the feeling evoked was the result of a careful manipulation of good elements of writing. They may not explain that awareness as successfully as a high school student would, but they are beginning to grasp the concepts and not just the personal reactions. They are beginning to differentiate between responding to the story itself and responding to a literary creation.

FOSTERING SELF-ESTEEM AND EMPATHY FOR OTHERS AND THE WORLD IN WHICH ONE LIVES

All-important is the use of literature as *bibliotherapy*. Literature allows the reader to identify with others and become aware of alternatives without feeling directly betrayed or threatened. For the high school student, the ability to empathize is an evaluative response and a much-desired outcome of literature studies.

Below is a list of books grouped by theme for discussion or writing. The titles are not grouped by reading level.

ABUSE:

⊙ Blair, Maury and Brendel, Doug. *Maury; Wednesday's Child*
⊙ Dizenzo, Patricia. *Why Me?*
⊙ Parrot, Andrea. *Coping with Date Rape and Acquaintance Rape*

NATURAL WORLD CONCERNS:

⊙ Caduto, M. and Bruchac, J. *Keepers of Earth*
⊙ Gay, Kathlyn. *Greenhouse Effect*
⊙ Johnson, Daenis. *Fiskadaro*
⊙ Madison, Arnold. *It Can't Happen to Me*

EATING DISORDERS:

⊙ Arnold, Caroline. *Too Fat, Too Thin, Do I Have a Choice?*
⊙ DeClements, Barthe. *Nothing's Fair in Fifth Grade*
⊙ Snyder, Anne. *Goodbye, Paper Doll*

FAMILY:

⊙ Chopin, Kate. *The Runner*
⊙ Cormier, Robert. *Tunes for Bears to Dance to*
⊙ Danzinger, Paula. *The Divorce Express*
⊙ Neufield, John. *Sunday Father*
⊙ Okimoto, Jean Davies. *Molly by any Other Name*
⊙ Peck, Richard. *Don't Look and It Won't Hurt*
⊙ Zindel, Paul. *I Never Loved Your Mind*

STEREOTYPING:

⊙ Baklanov, Grigory. (Trans. by Antonina W. Bouis) *Forever Nineteen*
⊙ Kerr, M.E. *Gentle Hands*
⊙ Greene, Betty. *Summer of My German Soldier*
⊙ Reiss, Johanna. *The Upstairs Room*
⊙ Taylor, Mildred D. *Roll of Thunder, Hear My Cry*
⊙ Wakatsuki-Houston, Jeanne and Houston, James D. *Farewell to Manzanar*

SUICIDE AND DEATH:

- ⊙ Blume, Judy. *Tiger Eyes*
- ⊙ Bunting, Eve. *If I Asked You, Would You Stay?*
- ⊙ Gunther, John. *Death Be Not Proud*
- ⊙ Mazer, Harry. *When the Phone Rings*
- ⊙ Peck, Richard. *Remembering the Good Times*
- ⊙ Richter, Elizabeth. *Losing Someone You Love*
- ⊙ Strasser, Todd. *Friends Till the End*

Cautions

Use caution when reading books containing sensitive subject matter. The teacher must be cognizant of the happenings in the school and outside community to spare students undue suffering. A child who has known a recent death in his family or circle of friends may need to distance himself from classroom discussion. Control any discussion to avoid students' pain or embarrassment.

Older children and young adults will be able to discuss issues with greater objectivity and without making insensitive comments. The teacher must be able to gauge the level of emotional development of his or her students when selecting subject matter and strategies for teaching. A student or parent may consider some material objectionable. Should a student choose not to read an assigned text, it is the teacher's responsibility to allow the student to select an alternate title. It is always advisable to notify parents if a particularly sensitive piece is to be studied. All literature should be approved by your administration.

COMPARING TEXTS

Fiction is the opposite of fact, and, simple as that may seem, it's the major distinction between works of fiction and works of fact.

Some (not all) types of nonfiction:

- ⊙ Almanac
- ⊙ Autobiography
- ⊙ Biography
- ⊙ Blueprint
- ⊙ Book report
- ⊙ Diary
- ⊙ Dictionary
- ⊙ Documentary film
- ⊙ Encyclopedia
- ⊙ Essay
- ⊙ History
- ⊙ Journal
- ⊙ Letter

- ⊙ Philosophy
- ⊙ Science book
- ⊙ Textbook
- ⊙ User manual

These can also be called **genres** of nonfiction—divisions of a particular art form according to criteria particular to that form. How these divisions are formed is vague. There are actually no fixed boundaries for either fiction or nonfiction. They are formed by sets of conventions, and many works cross into multiple genres by way of borrowing and recombining these conventions.

Some (not all) genres of fiction:

- ⊙ Action-adventure
- ⊙ Crime
- ⊙ Detective
- ⊙ Erotica
- ⊙ Fantasy
- ⊙ Horror
- ⊙ Mystery
- ⊙ Romance
- ⊙ Science fiction
- ⊙ Thriller
- ⊙ Western

A work of fiction typically has a central character, called the **protagonist**, and a character that stands in opposition, called the **antagonist**. The antagonist might be something other than a person. In Stephen Crane's short story, *The Open Boat*, for example, the antagonist is a hostile environment, a stormy sea. Conflicts between protagonist and antagonist are typical of a work of fiction, and the climax is the point at which those conflicts are resolved. The plot is the form or shape that the conflicts take as they move toward resolution.

A fiction writer uses **characterization** to reveal the personality of a character. This can be done directly or indirectly. In direct characterization, the writer tells readers directly what a character is like—for example, evil, sneaky, or brave. Indirect characterization is a method that reveals the character through the character's own words, thoughts, feelings, or actions and through the comments made by other characters.

One type of novel is the *bildungsroman* (from the German). It means "novel of education" or "novel of formation" and is a novel that traces the spiritual, moral, psychological, or social development and growth of the main character from childhood to maturity. Dickens' *David Copperfield* (1850) represents this genre, as does Thomas Wolfe's *Look Homeward Angel* (1929).

Enjoying fiction depends upon the reader's ability to suspend belief to some extent. The reader makes a deal with the writer that, for the time it takes to read the story, his or her own belief will be put aside, replaced by the convictions and reality that the writer has written into the story. This is not true in nonfiction. The writer of nonfiction declares in the choice of that genre that the work is based upon reality. The *MLA Style Manual*, for instance, can be relied upon because it is not the result of someone's imagination.

Skill 1.3   Identifying and analyzing figurative language and other literary elements

Plot is the series of events that make up a story. Most plots include an introduction or *exposition*; *rising action,* which includes complications; a *climax,* the most exciting point in the story; and the *resolution.*

If the plot does not move, the story quickly dies. Therefore, the successful writer of stories uses a wide variety of active verbs in creative and unusual ways. William Faulkner is a good example of a successful writer whose stories are lively and memorable because of his use of unusual active verbs.

Not all stories follow this traditional plot structure. Modern writers have experimented with how to reveal the plot, sometimes eliminating some or all parts to focus on other elements of the story.

Character is a person or animal in a story, play, or even poem. Characters are either *static* or *dynamic*. A *static character* does not change much throughout a story. A *dynamic character* changes as a result of the story's events or action. Characters are sometimes described also as *round* and *flat*. A *round character* is multifaceted while a *flat character* displays only one or limited sides of his or her development. Static characters sometimes appear stereotypical. A good test of characterization is the level of emotional involvement of the reader in the character.

(See Skill 1.2 Characterization)

Setting is the time and place of the story, play, or narrative poem. Setting may be visual, temporal, psychological, or social. Descriptive words are important to developing setting. In Edgar Allan Poe's description of the house in "The Fall of the House of Usher" as the protagonist/narrator approaches it, the air of dread and gloom that pervades the story is caught in the setting and sets the stage for the story. A setting may also be symbolic, as it is in Poe's story, where the house is a symbol of the family that lives in it. As the house disintegrates, so does the family.

The language used in all of these aspects of a story—plot, character, and setting—work together to create the **mood** of a story. Poe's first sentence establishes the mood:

> *During the whole of a dull, dark, and soundless day in the autumn of the year, when the clouds hung oppressively low in the heavens, I had been passing alone, on horseback, through a singularly dreary tract of country; and at length found myself, as the shades of the evening drew on, within view of the melancholy House of Usher.*

Essential terminology and literary devices germane to literary analysis include alliteration, allusion, antithesis, aphorism, apostrophe, assonance, blank verse, caesura, conceit, connotation, consonance, couplet, denotation, diction, epiphany, exposition, figurative language, free verse, hyperbole, iambic pentameter, inversion, irony, kenning, metaphor, metaphysical poetry, metonymy, motif, onomatopoeia, octava rima, oxymoron, paradox, parallelism, personification, quatrain, scansion, simile, soliloquy, Spenserian stanza, synecdoche, terza rima, tone, and wit.

The more basic terms and devices, such as alliteration, allusion, analogy, aside, assonance, atmosphere, climax, consonance, denouement, elegy, foil, foreshadowing, metaphor, simile, setting, symbol, and theme are defined and exemplified in the English 5–9 Study Guide.

LITERARY TERMS

Below are definitions of some of the more advanced terms.

Anachronism: Something or someone that is not in its correct historical or chronological time period.

Antithesis: Balanced writing about conflicting ideas, usually expressed in sentence form. Some examples are expanding from the center, shedding old habits, and searching never finding.

Aphorism: A focused, succinct expression about life from a sagacious viewpoint. Writings by Ben Franklin, Sir Francis Bacon, and Alexander Pope contain many aphorisms. "Whatever is begun in anger ends in shame" is an aphorism.

Apostrophe: Literary device of addressing an absent or dead person, an abstract idea, or an inanimate object. Sonneteers, such as Sir Thomas Wyatt, John Keats, and William Wordsworth, address the moon, stars, and the dead Milton. For example, in William Shakespeare's *Julius Caesar* Mark Antony addresses the corpse of Caesar in the speech that begins: "O, pardon me, thou bleeding piece of earth, / That I am meek and gentle with these butchers! / Thou art the ruins of the noblest man / That ever lived in the tide of times. / Woe to the hand that shed this costly blood!"

Blank Verse: Poetry written in unrhymed iambic pentameter. Works by Shakespeare and Milton are epitomes of blank verse. Milton's *Paradise Lost* states, "Illumine, what is low raise and support, / That to the highth of this great argument / I may assert Eternal Providence / And justify the ways of God to men."

Caesura: A pause, usually signaled by punctuation, in a line of poetry. The earliest usage occurs in *Beowulf*, the first English epic dating from the Anglo-Saxon era. An example of a caesura is "To err is human, // to forgive, divine" (Pope).

Conceit: A comparison, usually in verse, between seemingly disparate objects or concepts. John Donne's metaphysical poetry contains many clever conceits. For instance, Donne's "The Flea" (1633) compares a flea bite to the act of love; and in "A Valediction: Forbidding Mourning" (1633) separated lovers are likened to the legs of a compass, the leg drawing the circle eventually returning home to "the fixed foot."

Connotation: The implications and associations of a given word, distinct from the denotative, or literal, meaning. For example, "Good night, sweet prince; And flights of angels sing thee to thy rest" refers to a burial.

Consonance: The repeated usage of similar consonant sounds, most often used in poetry. For example: roam, same; birth, death.

Couplet: Two rhyming lines of poetry. A heroic couplet is a couplet written in rhymed iambic pentameter. Shakespeare's sonnets end in heroic couplets. Pope is also a master of the couplet. His *Rape of the Lock* is written entirely in heroic couplets.

Denotation: The literal or dictionary definition of a word as opposed to the connotative meaning. For example, "Good night, sweet prince; And flights of angels sing thee to thy *rest*" refers to sleep.

Diction: The choice of words or phrases that a writer uses to help create meaning. Formal diction is elevated or dignified and often creates a lofty tone. Middle diction is less elevated and is how most people speak. Informal diction is plain, everyday language and often includes slang and simple, common words.

Epiphany: When a character suddenly makes a deep realization about himself or discovers a truth about life.

Exposition: The beginning of a story or literary work that provides the background information about the characters, setting, and plot.

Figurative Language: Language not meant in a literal sense but rather to suggest additional meaning or effect. Figurative language is made up of such literary devices as hyperbole, metonymy, synecdoche, and oxymoron.

Free Verse: Poetry that does not have any predictable meter or patterning. Margaret Atwood, e. e. cummings, and Ted Hughes write in this form.

Hyperbole: Exaggeration for a specific effect. For example, "I'm so hungry that I could eat a million of these."

Iambic Pentameter: The two elements in a set five-foot line of poetry. An *iamb* is two syllables, unaccented and accented, per foot or measure. *Pentameter* means five feet of these iambs per line or ten syllables.

Inversion: Inversion is a typical sentence order to create a given effect or interest. Bacon and Milton's work use inversion successfully. Emily Dickinson was fond of arranging words outside of their familiar order. For example, in "Chartless" she writes, "Yet know I how the heather looks" and "Yet certain am I of the spot." Instead of saying "Yet I know" and "Yet I am certain" she reverses the usual order and shifts the emphasis to the more important words.

Irony: An unexpected disparity between what is written or stated and what is really meant or implied by the author. Verbal, situational, and dramatic are the three types of literary irony. *Verbal irony* is when an author says one thing and means something else. *Dramatic irony* is when an audience or reader knows something that the character does not know. *Situational irony* is a discrepancy between the expected result and actual result. Shakespeare's plays contain numerous and highly effective use of irony. O. Henry's short stories have ironic endings.

Kenning: Another way to describe a person, place, or thing so as to avoid prosaic repetition. The earliest examples can be found in Anglo-Saxon literature such as *Beowulf* and "The Seafarer." Instead of writing "King Hrothgar," the anonymous monk wrote "great Ring-Giver, or Father of his people." A lake becomes "the swans' way," and the ocean or sea becomes "the great whale's way." In ancient Greek literature this device was called an "epithet."

Metaphysical Poetry: Verse characterized by ingenious wit, unparalleled imagery, and clever conceits. The greatest metaphysical poet is John Donne. Henry Vaughn and other seventeeth-century British poets contributed to this movement; for example, in *Words*, "I saw eternity the other night, like a great being of pure and endless light."

Metonymy: Use of an object or idea closely identified with another object or idea to represent the latter. "Hit the books" means "go study." Washington, D.C. means the U.S. government and the White House means the U.S. President.

Motif: A key, oft-repeated phrase, name, or idea in or across literary works. Dorset/Wessex in Hardy's novels and the moors and the harsh weather in the Bronte sisters' novels are effective uses of motifs. Shakespeare's *Romeo and Juliet* represents the ill-fated young lovers motif.

Onomatopoeia: Word used to evoke the sound in its meaning. The early Batman series used *pow, zap, whop, zonk,* and *eek* in an onomatopoetic way.

Octava rima: A specific eight-line stanza of poetry with a rhyme scheme of abababcc. Lord Byron's mock epic, *Don Juan,* is written in octava rima.

Oxymoron: A contradictory form of speech, such as jumbo shrimp, unkindly kind, or singer John Mellencamp's "It hurts so good."

Paradox: A seemingly untrue statement, which when examined more closely proves to be true. John Donne's sonnet "Death Be Not Proud" postulates that death shall die and humans will triumph over death—at first this seems untrue but it is ultimately explained and proven in this sonnet.

Parody: A humorous imitation of a literary or other artistic work.

Parallelism: Using the same grammatical structures or patterns of words to show a balance in meaning or sound. The psalms in the King James Version of the Bible contain many examples.

Personification: Giving human characteristics to inanimate objects or concepts. Great writers, with few exceptions, are masters of this literary device.

Quatrain: A poetic stanza composed of four lines. A Shakespearean or Elizabethan sonnet is made up of three quatrains and ends with a heroic couplet.

Scansion: The two-part analysis of a poetic line. To scan a poem, count the number of syllables per line and determine where the accents fall. Divide the line into metric feet. Name the meter by the type and number of feet. Much is written about scanning poetry. Try not to inundate your students with this jargon; allow them to feel the power of the poets' words, ideas, and images instead.

Soliloquy: A highlighted speech, in drama, usually delivered by a major character expounding on the author's philosophy or expressing, at times, universal truths. This is done with the character alone on the stage.

Synecdoche: A metaphor in which the word for part of something is used to mean the whole; for example, "sail" for "boat," or vice versa. Another example is calling a vehicle "wheels."

Spenserian stanza: Invented by Sir Edmund Spenser and used in *The Fairie Queene*, his epic poem honoring Queen Elizabeth I. Each stanza consists of nine lines, eight in iambic parameter. The ninth line, called an *alexandrine*, has two extra syllables or one additional foot.

Sprung rhythm: Invented and used extensively by the poet Gerard Manley Hopkins. It consists of variable meter, which combines stressed and unstressed syllables fashioned by the author. See "Pied Beauty" or "God's Grandeur."

Stream of consciousness: A style of writing that reflects the mental processes of the characters expressing, at times, jumbled memories, feelings, and dreams. Authors using stream of consciousness include James Joyce, Virginia Woolf, and William Faulkner.

Terza rima: A series of poetic stanzas utilizing the recurrent rhyme scheme of aba, bcb, cdc, ded, and so forth. The second-generation Romantic poets—Keats, Byron, Shelley, and, to a lesser degree, Yeats—used this Italian verse form, especially in their odes. Dante used terza rima in *The Divine Comedy*.

Tone: The author's attitude toward the subject, readership, or characters. Swift's tone and Pope's tone are satirical. Boswell's tone toward Johnson is admiring.

Wit: Writing of genius, keenness, and sagacity expressed through clever use of language. Alexander Pope and the Augustans wrote about and were themselves said to possess wit.

POETIC ELEMENTS

Slant or approximate rhyme: The rhyme is almost but not exactly the same. It occurs when the final consonant sounds are the same but the vowels are different. Slant rhyme occurs frequently in Irish, Welsh, and Icelandic verse. Examples include: green and gone, that and hit, ill and shell.

Alliteration: Alliteration occurs when the initial sounds of a word, beginning either with a consonant or a vowel, are repeated in close succession. Examples include: Athena and Apollo, Nate never knows, People who pen poetry.

Note that the words only have to be close to one another: Alliteration that repeats and attempts to connect a number of words is little more than a tongue-twister.

The function of alliteration, like rhyme, might be to accentuate the beauty of language in a given context or to unite words or concepts through a kind of repetition. Alliteration, like rhyme, can follow specific patterns. Sometimes the consonants aren't always the initial consonants of the words, but they are generally the stressed syllables.

Alliteration is less common than rhyme, but because it is less common it can call attention to a word or line in a poem that might not have the same emphasis otherwise.

Assonance: If alliteration occurs at the beginning of a word and rhyme at the end, assonance takes the middle territory. Assonance occurs when the vowel sound within a word matches the same sound in a nearby word but the surrounding consonant sounds are different. "Tune" and "June" are rhymes; "tune" and "food" are assonant. The function of assonance is frequently the same as rhyme or alliteration; all serve to give a sense of continuity or fluidity to the verse. Assonance can be especially effective when rhyme is absent. It gives the poet more flexibility and it is not typically used as part of a predetermined pattern. Like alliteration, it does not so much determine the structure or form of a poem; rather, it is more ornamental.

Imagery can be described as a word or sequence of words that refers to any sensory experience—that is, anything that can be seen, tasted, smelled, heard, or felt on the skin or with the fingers. While writers of prose may also use these devices, it is most distinctive of poetry. The poet intends to make an experience available to the reader. In order to do that, he or she must appeal to one of the senses. The most common type of imagery is visual imagery. The poet will deliberately paint a scene in such a way that the reader can "see" it. However, the purpose is not simply to stir a visceral feeling but also to stir the reader's emotions. A good example is "The Piercing Chill" by Taniguchi Buson (1715–1783):

> The piercing chill I feel:
> My dead wife's comb, in our bedroom,
> Under my heel . . .

In a few short words, the reader can feel many things: the shock that might come from touching a corpse, a literal sense of death, and the contrast between her death and the memories he has of her when she was alive. Imagery can be defined as speaking of the abstract in concrete terms and is a powerful device in the hands of a skillful poet.

A **symbol** is an object, person, or image that elicits additional meaning beyond its literal meaning. Symbols are often abstract. Conventional symbols have meanings that are widely recognized by a culture or society. For example, the lion is a symbol of courage; the cross a symbol of Christianity; and the color green is a symbol of envy. Symbols used in literature are often of a different sort. They tend to be private and personal and their significance is only evident in the context of the work where they are used. A good example is the huge pair of spectacles on a billboard in Fitzgerald's *The Great Gatsby*. They are interesting as a part of the landscape, but they also symbolize divine myopia.

A symbol can certainly have more than one meaning and the meaning can be as personal as the memories and experiences of the particular reader. In analyzing a poem or a story it's important to identify the symbols and their possible meanings.

> **Teaching Tip**: *Looking for symbols is often challenging, especially for novice poetry readers. However, these suggestions may be useful. First, pick out all the references to concrete objects such as a newspaper, black cats, etc. Note any that the poet emphasizes by describing in detail, by repeating, or by placing at the very beginning or end of a poem. Ask yourself, what is the poem about? What does it add up to? Paraphrase the poem and determine whether or not the meaning depends upon certain concrete objects. Then ponder what the concrete object symbolizes in the poem. Look for a character with the name of a prophet who does little but utter prophecy or a trio of women who resemble the Three Fates. A symbol may be a part of a person's body such as the eye of the murder victim in Poe's story "The Tell-Tale Heart" or a look, a voice, or a mannerism.*

Allusion: A reference to a person, place, thing, event, or idea in history or literature. Allusions are based on the assumption that there is a common body of knowledge shared by the poet and the reader and that a reference to that body of knowledge will be immediately understood. Allusions to the Bible, Shakespeare, and classical mythology are common in Western literature on the assumption that they will be immediately understood.

This is not always the case, of course. T. S. Eliot's *The Waste Land* requires research and annotation for understanding. He assumed far more background than the average reader has. However, when Michael Moore on his website headlined an article on the war in Iraq: "Déjà Fallouja: Ramadi surrounded, thousands of families trapped, no electricity or water, onslaught impending," we understand immediately that he is referring first of all to a repeat of the human disaster in New Orleans during Hurricane Katrina, although the "onslaught" is not a storm but an invasion by American and Iraqi troops.

The use of allusion is a sort of shortcut for poets. They can use an economy of words and count on meaning to come from the reader's own experience.

Figurative language is also called *figures of speech*. If all figures of speech that have ever been identified were listed, it would be a very long list. However, for purposes of analyzing poetry, a few are sufficient.

1. **Simile**: Direct comparison between two things. For example, "My love is like a red-red rose."
2. **Metaphor**: Indirect comparison between two things. The use of a word or phrase denoting one kind of object or action in place of another to suggest

a comparison between them. While poets use metaphors extensively, they are also integral to everyday speech.

3. **Parallelism**: The arrangement of ideas in phrases, sentences, and paragraphs that balance one element with another of equal importance and similar wording. An example from Francis Bacon's *Of Studies*: "Reading maketh a full man, conference a ready man, and writing an exact man."

4. **Personification**: Human characteristics attributed to an inanimate object, an abstract quality, or an animal. Examples: John Bunyan included characters named Death, Knowledge, Giant Despair, Sloth, and Piety in his *Pilgrim's Progress*. The metaphor of an arm of a chair is a form of personification.

5. **Euphemism**: The substitution of an agreeable or inoffensive term for one that might offend or suggest something unpleasant. Many euphemisms are used to refer to death to avoid using the real word, such as "passed away," "crossed over," or "passed."

6. **Hyperbole**: Deliberate exaggeration for effect or comic effect. The following example is from Shakespeare's *The Merchant of Venice*:

> *Why, if two gods should play some heavenly match*
> *And on the wager lay two earthly women,*
> *And Portia one, there must be something else*
> *Pawned with the other, for the poor rude world*
> *Hath not her fellow.*

7. **Climax**: A number of phrases or sentences are arranged in ascending order of rhetorical forcefulness. The following example is from Melville's *Moby-Dick*:

> *All that most maddens and torments; all that stirs up the lees of things; all truth with malice in it; all that cracks the sinews and cakes the brain; all the subtle demonisms of life and thought; all evil, to crazy Ahab, were visibly personified and made practically assailable in Moby Dick.*

8. **Bathos**: A ludicrous attempt to portray pathos—that is, to evoke pity, sympathy, or sorrow. It may result from inappropriately dignifying the commonplace, elevated language to describe something trivial, or greatly exaggerated pathos.

9. **Irony**: Expressing something other than and or opposite the literal meaning, such as words of praise when blame is intended. In poetry, it is often used as a sophisticated or resigned awareness of contrast between what is and what ought to be and expresses a controlled pathos without sentimentality.

10. **Alliteration**: (See Poetic Elements above.)

11. **Onomatopoeia**: (See Literary Terms above.)

12. **Malapropism**: A verbal blunder in which one word is replaced by another similar in sound but different in meaning. The term comes from Sheridan's Mrs. Malaprop in *The Rivals* (1775). Thinking of the geography of contiguous countries, she spoke of the "geometry" of "contagious countries."

The Value of Figurative Language

Poets use figures of speech to sharpen the effect and meaning of their poems and to help readers see things in ways they have never seen them before. Marianne Moore observed that a fir tree has "an emerald turkey-foot at the top." Her poem makes us aware of something we probably had never noticed before. The sudden recognition of the likeness yields pleasure in reading. Figurative language allows for the statement of truths that more literal language cannot. Skillfully used, a figure of speech will help the reader see more clearly and focus upon particulars. Figures of speech add richness to our reading and understanding of a poem and they allow opportunities for worthwhile analysis.

Skill 1.4 Identifying patterns, structures, and characteristics of literary forms and genres

MAJOR LITERARY GENRES

Allegory: A story in verse or prose in which the characters, setting, and events stand for other people, events, and ideas. There are two meanings to the text, symbolic and literal. John Bunyan's *The Pilgrim's Progress* is the most renowned of this genre.

Ballad: An *in medias res* story told or sung, usually in verse and accompanied by music. Literary devices found in ballads include the *refrain*, or repeated section, and incremental repetition, or *anaphora*, for effect. Earliest forms were anonymous folk ballads. Later forms include Coleridge's Romantic masterpiece, *The Rime of the Ancient Mariner*.

Drama: Plays—comedy, modern, or tragedy—typically in five acts. Traditionalists and neoclassicists adhere to Aristotle's unities of time, place, and action. Plot development is advanced through dialogue. Literary devices include asides, soliloquies, and the chorus representing public opinion. Greatest of all dramatists/playwrights is William Shakespeare. Other dramaturges include Ibsen, Williams, Miller, Shaw, Stoppard, Racine, Moliére, Sophocles, Aeschylus, Euripides, and Aristophanes.

Epic: A long poem usually of book length reflecting values inherent in the generative society. Epic devices include an invocation to a Muse for inspiration, purpose for writing, universal setting, protagonist and antagonist who possess supernatural strength and acumen, and interventions of a God or the gods.

Understandably, there are very few epics: Homer's *Iliad* and *Odyssey*, Virgil's *Aeneid*, Milton's *Paradise Lost*, Spenser's *The Fairie Queene*, Barrett Browning's *Aurora Leigh*, and Pope's mock-epic, *The Rape of the Lock*.

Epistle: A letter that is not always originally intended for public distribution, but due to the fame of the sender and/or recipient, becomes public domain. Paul wrote epistles that were later placed in the Bible.

Essay: Typically a limited-length prose work focusing on a topic and propounding a definite point of view and written using an authoritative tone. Great essayists include Carlyle, Lamb, DeQuincy, Emerson, and Montaigne, who is credited with defining this genre.

Fable: Terse tale offering a moral or exemplum. Chaucer's "The Nun's Priest's Tale" is a fine example of a *bete fabliau* or beast fable in which animals speak and act characteristically human, illustrating human foibles.

Legend: A traditional narrative or collection of related narratives, popularly regarded as historically factual but actually a mixture of fact and fiction.

Myth: Stories that are universally shared within a culture to explain its history and traditions.

Novel: The longest form of fictional prose containing a variety of characterizations, settings, local color, and regionalism. Most have complex plots, expanded description, and attention to detail. Some of the great novelists include Austin, the Brontes, Twain, Tolstoy, Hugo, Hardy, Dickens, Hawthorne, Forster, and Flaubert.

Poem: Rhythmic, compressed language that uses figures of speech and imagery to appeal to the readers' emotions and imaginations. Subgenres include sonnet, elegy, ode, pastoral, villanelle, and free verse.

Romance: A highly imaginative tale set in a fantastical realm dealing with the conflicts between heroes, villains, and/or monsters. "The Knight's Tale" from Chaucer's *Canterbury Tales*, *Sir Gawain and the Green Knight* and Keats' "The Eve of St. Agnes" are prime representatives.

Short Story: Typically a terse fictional prose narrative that is ten to twenty pages in length. Poe emphasized that a successful short story should create one focused impact. Great short story writers include Hemingway, Faulkner, Twain, Joyce, Shirley Jackson, Flannery O'Connor, de Maupasssant, Saki, Edgar Allen Poe, and Pushkin.

Types of Drama

Comedy: The comedic form of dramatic literature is meant to amuse and often ends happily. Comedy uses techniques such as satire or parody and can take many forms, from farce to burlesque. Examples include Dante Alighieri's *The Divine Comedy,* Noel Coward's play *Private Lives,* some of Geoffrey Chaucer's *Canterbury Tales*, and some of William Shakespeare's plays.

Tragedy: Tragedy is comedy's other half. It is a story involving courageous characters who confront strong forces in or outside themselves with dignity that illustrates the depth of human spirit in the face of failure. It is characterized by serious, poetic language that evokes pity and fear. Traditionally, a tragedy involved a character of high standing who possessed a character flaw that caused his downfall. In modern times, dramatists have tried to update the image of tragedy by drawing its main characters from the middle class and showing their nobility through their nature instead of their standing. The classic example of tragedy is Sophocles' *Oedipus Rex*, while Henrik Ibsen and Arthur Miller epitomize modern tragedy.

Drama: In its most general sense, a drama is any work intended to be performed by actors onstage. Drama can also refer to the broad literary genre that includes comedy and tragedy. Contemporary usage, however, denotes drama as a work that treats serious subjects and themes but does not aim for the same grandeur as tragedy.

Drama usually deals with characters of a less stately nature than tragedy does. A classical example of tragedy is Sophocles' *Oedipus Rex,* while Eugene O'Neill's *The Iceman Cometh* represents modern drama.

Dramatic monologue: A dramatic monologue is a speech given by an actor, usually intended for him- or herself, but with the intended audience in mind. It reveals key aspects of the character's psyche and sheds insight on the situation at hand. The audience takes the part of the silent listener, passing judgment and giving sympathy at the same time. This form was invented and used predominantly by Victorian poet Robert Browning.

Tempo: The timing and interpretation of dialogue. The dialogue must be connected to motivation and detail. While interpreting the dialogue and actions, the director is also concerned with pace and seeks a variation of tempo. If the overall pace is too slow, then the action becomes dull and dragging. If the overall pace is too fast, then the audience will not be able to understand what is going on because they are being hit with too much information to process.

Dramatic arc: Good drama is built on conflict of some kind—an opposition of forces or desires that must be resolved by the end of the story. The conflict can be internal, involving emotional and psychological pressures, or it can be external, drawing the characters into tumultuous events. These conflicts are presented to the audience in a narrative arc that looks roughly like this:

Climax

Intro | Conflict development | Resolution

Following the arc

Although any performance may have a series of rising and falling levels of intensity, in general the opening should set in motion the events that will generate an emotional high toward the middle or end of the story. Then, regardless of whether the ending is happy, sad, bittersweet, or despairing, the resolution eases the audience down from those heights and establishes some sense of closure. Reaching the climax too soon undermines the dramatic impact of the remaining portion of the performance, whereas reaching it too late rushes the ending and creates a jarringly abrupt end to events.

Types of Nonfiction

Biography: A form of nonfiction, the subject of which is the life of an individual. The earliest biographical writings were probably funeral speeches and inscriptions, usually praising the life and example of the deceased. Early biographies evolved from this and were almost always uncritical, even distorted, and always laudatory.

Autobiography: A form of biography written by the subject himself or herself. Autobiographies can range from very formal to intimate writings made during the subject's life that were not intended for publication. These include letters, diaries, journals, memoirs, and reminiscences. There are four kinds of autobiography: thematic, religious, intellectual, and fictionalized. Some "novels" may be thinly disguised autobiography, such as the novels of Thomas Wolfe.

Informational books and articles: This genre makes up much of the reading of modern Americans. Magazines began to be popular in the nineteenth century in this country, and while many of the contributors to those publications intended to influence the political, social, or religious convictions of their readers, many also simply intended to pass on information. A book or article whose purpose is simply to be informative, that is, not to persuade, is called *exposition* (adjectival form: expository). An example of an expository book is the *MLA Style Manual*. The writers do not intend to persuade their readers to use the recommended stylistic features in their writing; they are simply making them available in case a reader needs such a guide. Articles in magazines such as *Time* may be persuasive in purpose, such as Joe Klein's regular column, but for the most part they are expository, giving information that television coverage of a news story might not have time to include.

Newspaper accounts of events: Newspapers are expository in nature and report something that has happened. They are not intended to be persuasive although the bias of a reporter or an editor must be considered. A newspaper's editorial stance is often openly declared and it may be reflected in such things as news reports. Reporters are expected to be unbiased in their coverage and most of them will defend their disinterest fiercely. However, what a writer *sees* in an event is inevitably shaped to some extent by the writer's beliefs and experiences.

Types of Poetry

Sonnet: The sonnet is a fixed-verse form of Italian origin, which consists of 14 lines that are typically five-foot iambics rhyming according to a prescribed scheme. Popular since its creation in the thirteenth century in Sicily, it spread at first to Tuscany, where it was adopted by Petrarch. The *Petrarchan sonnet* generally has a two-part theme. The first eight lines, the octave, state a problem, ask a question, or express an emotional tension. The last six lines, the sestet, resolve the problem, answer the question, or relieve the tension. The rhyme scheme of the octave is abbaabba; that of the sestet varies.

The *English sonnet* is composed of three quatrains, each with an independent rhyme scheme, and it ends with a rhymed couplet. A form of the English sonnet created by Edmond Spenser combines the English form and the Italian. The *Spenserian sonnet* follows the English quatrain and couplet pattern but resembles the Italian in its rhyme scheme, which is linked: abab bcbc cdcd ee. Many poets wrote sonnet sequences, in which several sonnets were linked together, usually to tell a story.

Considered to be the greatest of all sonnet sequences is one of Shakespeare's, which is addressed to a young man and a "dark lady" wherein the love story is overshadowed by the underlying reflections on time and art, growth and decay, and fame and fortune.

John Donne, in the seventeenth century, used the form for religious themes, some of which are almost sermons, or on personal reflections ("When I consider how my light is spent").

That the sonnet is a flexible form is demonstrated in the wide range of themes and purposes for which it has been used—from frivolous concerns to statements about time and death. Wordsworth, Keats, and Elizabeth Barrett Browning used the Petrarchan form of the sonnet. A well-known example is Wordsworth's "The World Is Too Much With Us." Rainer Maria Rilke's *Sonnette an Orpheus* (1922) is a well-known twentieth-century sonnet.

Teaching Tip: *Analysis of a sonnet should focus on the form—does it fit a traditional pattern or does it break from tradition? If it breaks from tradition, why did the poet choose to make that break? Does it reflect the purpose of the poem? What is the theme? What is the purpose? Is it narrative? If so, what story does it tell and is there an underlying meaning? Is the sonnet appropriate for the subject matter?*

Limerick: The limerick probably originated in County Limerick, Ireland, in the eighteenth century. It is a form of short, humorous verse, often nonsensical and often ribald. Its five lines rhyme aabbaa with three feet in all lines except the third and fourth, which have only two. Rarely presented as serious poetry, this form is popular because almost anyone can write it, although writing a truly good limerick is more challenging than it may at first seem.

Cinquain: A poem with a five-line stanza. Adelaide Crapsey (1878–1914) called a five-line verse form a *cinquain* and invented a particular meter for it. Similar to the haiku, there are two syllables in the first and last lines and four, six, and eight in the middle three lines. It has a mostly iambic cadence. Her poem, "November Night," is an example:

> *Listen…*
> *With faint dry sound*
> *Like steps of passing ghosts,*
> *the leaves, frost-crisp'd, break from the trees*
> *And fall.*

Haiku: A very popular unrhymed form that is limited to seventeen syllables arranged in three lines with five, seven, and five syllables, respectively. This verse form originated in Japan in the seventeenth century where it is accepted as serious poetry and is Japan's most popular poetic form. It was originally created to deal with the season, the time of day, and the landscape. However, it has come into more common use and the subjects have become less restricted.

Teaching Tip: *Analysis of a cinquain and a haiku poem should focus on form first. Does the haiku poem conform to the seventeen-syllable requirement and are they arranged in a five, seven, and five pattern? For a cinquain, does it have only five lines? Does the poem distill the words so as much meaning as possible can be conveyed? Does it treat a serious subject? Is the theme discernable? Short forms like these seem simple to dash off; however, they are not effective unless the words are chosen and pared so the meaning intended is conveyed. The impact should be forceful, and that often takes more effort, skill, and creativity than longer forms of poetry require.*

Other forms of poetry include:

- ⊙ Villanelle
- ⊙ Sestina
- ⊙ Ballad
- ⊙ Epic
- ⊙ Narrative
- ⊙ Free verse
- ⊙ Rondeau
- ⊙ Elegy
- ⊙ Ode
- ⊙ Concrete or visual
- ⊙ Pastoral

ANALYZING POETRY

Narrative Poetry: The greatest difficulty in analyzing narrative poetry is that it partakes of many genres. It can have all the features of poetry: meter, rhyme, verses, stanzas, etc., but it can also have all the features of prose, not only fictional prose but also nonfiction. It can have a protagonist, characters, conflicts, action, plot, climax, theme, and tone. It can also be a persuasive discourse and have a thesis (real or derived) and supporting points. The arrangement of an analysis will depend to a great extent upon the peculiarities of the poem itself.

Epic Poem: In an epic, the conflicts take place in the social sphere rather than in a personal life, and an epic will have a historical basis or one that is accepted as historical. The conflict will be between opposing nations or races and will involve diverging views of civilization that are the foundation of the challenge. Often it will involve the pitting of a group that conceives of itself as a higher civilization against a lower civilization and, more often than not, divine will determines that the higher civilization will win, exerting its force over the lower, barbarous, and profane enemy. Examples are the conflict of Greece with Troy, the fates of Rome with the Carthaginian and the Italian, the Crusaders with the Saracen, or even of Milton's Omnipotent versus Satan. In analyzing these works, protagonist and antagonist need to be clearly identified, the conflicts established, and the climax and an outcome that sets the world right clearly shown.

At the same time, the form of the epic as a poem must be considered. What meter, rhyme scheme, verse form, and stanza form have been chosen to tell this story? Is the form consistent? If it varies, where does it vary and what does the varying do for the epic? What about figures of speech? Is there alliteration or onomatopoeia? It is important to examine these and other questions of form.

The epic is historically a major literary form although it had begun to fall out of favor by the end of the seventeenth century. There have been notable efforts to produce an American epic, but they always seem to slide over into prose. The short story and the novel began to take over the genre. Even so, some would say that *Moby-Dick* is an American epic.

Fables and folktales: This literary group of stories and legends was originally transmitted orally to the common populace to provide models of exemplary behavior or deeds worthy of recognition and homage.

In fables, animals talk, feel, and behave like human beings. The fable always has a moral and the animals illustrate specific people or groups without directly identifying them. For example, in Aesop's *Fables,* the lion is the "King" and the wolf is the cruel, often unfeeling, "noble class." In the fable of "The Lion and the Mouse" the moral is that "Little friends may prove to be great friends." In "The Lion's Share" it is "Might makes right."

Many British folktales—*How Robin Became an Outlaw* and *St. George: Slaying of the Dragon*—stress the correlation between power and right.

Classical mythology: Much of the mythology that produces allusions in modern English writings is a product of ancient Greece and Rome because these myths have been widely translated. Some Norse myths are also well known. Children are fond of myths because the stories seek explanations for those elements that predated scientific knowledge just as children seek explanations for the occurrences in their lives.

Myths provide insight into the order and ethics of life as ancient heroes overcome the terrors of the unknown and bring meaning to the thunder and lightning, to the changing of the seasons, to the magical creatures of the forests and seas, and to the myriad of natural phenomena that can frighten mankind. There is often a childlike quality in the emotions of supernatural beings with which children can identify. Many good translations of myths exist for readers of varying abilities, but Edith Hamilton's *Mythology* is the most definitive reading for adolescents.

Fairy tales: Fairy tales are lively fictional stories involving children or animals that come in contact with supernatural beings via magic. They provide happy solutions to human dilemmas. The fairy tales of many nations are peopled by trolls, elves, dwarfs, and pixies, child-sized beings capable of fantastic accomplishments.

Among the most famous are "Beauty and the Beast," "Cinderella," "Hansel and Gretel," "Snow White and the Seven Dwarfs," "Rumplestiltskin," and "Tom Thumb." In each tale, the protagonist survives prejudice, imprisonment, ridicule, or even death to receive justice in a cruel world.

Older readers encounter a kind of fairy tale world in Shakespeare's *The Tempest* and *A Midsummer Night's Dream*, which use pixies and fairies as characters. Adolescent readers today are fascinated by the creations of fantasy realms in the works of Piers Anthony, Ursula LeGuin, and Anne McCaffrey. An extension of interest in the supernatural is the popularity of science fiction that allows writers to use current knowledge to predict the possible course of the future.

Biblical stories: Biblical stories provide many allusions. Parables, which are moralistic like fables but have human characters, include the stories of the Good Samaritan and the Prodigal Son. References to the treachery of Cain and the betrayal of Christ by Judas Iscariot are oft-cited examples.

American folk tales: American folktales are divided into two categories:

1. **Imaginary tales, also called tall tales:** Humorous tales based on non-existent, fictional characters developed through blatant exaggeration. There are many popular tall tale characters.

   ⊙ John Henry is a two-fisted steel driver who beats out a steam drill in competition.
   ⊙ Rip Van Winkle sleeps for twenty years in the Catskill Mountains and upon awakening cannot understand why no one recognizes him.
   ⊙ Paul Bunyan, a giant lumberjack, owns a great blue ox named Babe and has extraordinary physical strength. He is said to have plowed the Mississippi River while the impression of Babe's hoof prints created the Great Lakes.

2. **Real tales, also called legends:** Tales based on real persons who accomplished the feats that are attributed to them—even if they are slightly exaggerated. The following are common American legends.

   ⊙ For more than forty years, Johnny Appleseed (John Chapman) roamed Ohio and Indiana planting apple seeds.
   ⊙ Daniel Boone—scout, adventurer, and pioneer—blazed the Wilderness Trail and made Kentucky safe for settlers.
   ⊙ Paul Revere, a colonial patriot, rode through the New England countryside warning of the approach of British troops.
   ⊙ George Washington cut down a cherry tree, which he could not deny.

Skill 1.5   Situating and interpreting texts within their historical and cultural contexts

AMERICAN LITERATURE

Influences on American Literature

Local color

Local color is defined as presenting the peculiarities of a particular locality and its inhabitants. This genre appeared primarily after the Civil War although there were certainly precursors, such as Washington Irving and his depiction of life in the Catskill Mountains of New York. However, the local colorist movement is generally considered to have begun in 1865, when humor began to permeate the writing of those who were focusing on a particular region of the country.

Samuel L. Clemens (Mark Twain) is best known for his humorous works about the Southwest, such as *The Notorious Jumping Frog of Calaveras County*. The country had just emerged from its "long night of the soul," a time when death, despair, and disaster had preoccupied the nation for almost five years. It's no wonder that the artists sought to relieve the grief and pain and lift spirits nor is it surprising that their efforts brought such a strong response. Mark Twain is generally considered to be not only one of America's funniest writers but also one who also wrote great and enduring fiction.

Other examples of local colorists who used many of the same devices as Twain are Harriet Beecher Stowe, Bret Harte, George Washington Cable, Joel Chandler Harris, and Sarah Orne Jewett.

Slavery

The best known of the early writers who used fiction as a political statement about slavery is Harriet Beecher Stowe, author of *Uncle Tom's Cabin*. This was her first novel, and it was published first as a serial in 1851 then as a book in 1852. It brought an angry reaction from people living in the South.

This antislavery book infuriated Southerners. However, Stowe herself had been angered by the 1850 Fugitive Slave Law, which made it legal to indict those who assisted runaway slaves. It took away rights not only of the runaways but also of the free slaves. She intended to generate a protest of the law and slavery. Her novel was the first effort to present the lives of slaves from their standpoint. Stowe cleverly used depictions of motherhood and Christianity to stir her readers. When President Lincoln finally met her, he told her it was her book that started the Civil War.

Many writers used the printed word to protest slavery. Some of them include:

- Frederick Douglas
- William Lloyd Garrison
- Benjamin Lay, a Quaker
- Connecticut theologian Jonathan Edward
- Susan B. Anthony

Westward migration

This has been a popular topic for literature from the time of the Louisiana Purchase in 1804. The recent *Undaunted Courage* by Stephen E. Ambrose is ostensibly the autobiography of Meriwether Lewis but is actually a recounting of the Lewis and Clark expedition. Presented by President Jefferson as a scientific expedition, the expedition was also intended to provide maps and information for the opening up of the West. A well-known novel about the settling of the West by immigrants from other countries is *Giants in the Earth* by Ole Edvart Rolvaag, himself a descendant of immigrants.

Civil rights

Many abolitionists were also early crusaders for civil rights. However, the 1960s Civil Rights Movement focused attention on the plight of the people who had been "freed" by the Civil War in ways that brought about long overdue changes in the opportunities and rights of African Americans. David Halberstam, who had been a reporter in Nashville at the time of the sit-ins by eight young black college students that initiated the revolution, wrote *The Children*, published in 1998, to remind Americans of these students' courage, suffering, and achievements. Congressman John Lewis, Fifth District, Georgia, was one of those eight young men who has gone on to a life of public service. Halberstam records that when older black ministers tried to persuade these young people not to pursue their protest, John Lewis responded: "If not us, then who? If not now, then when?"

Some examples of civil rights protest literature include:

- James Baldwin, *Blues for Mister Charlie*
- Martin Luther King Jr., *Where Do We Go from Here?*
- Langston Hughes, *Fight for Freedom: The Story of the NAACP*
- Eldridge Cleaver, *Soul on Ice*
- Malcolm X, *The Autobiography of Malcolm X*
- Stokely Carmichael and Charles V. Hamilton, *Black Power*
- Leroi Jones, *Home*

Vietnam

An America that was already divided over the Civil Rights Movement faced even greater divisions over the war in Vietnam. Those who were in favor of the war and who opposed withdrawal saw it as the major front in the war against communism. Those who opposed the war and who favored withdrawal of the troops believed that it would not serve to defeat communism and was a quagmire.

The Things They Carried by Tim O'Brien, a Vietnam veteran, is a collection of related short stories about a platoon of American soldiers in the Vietnam War. *Authors Take Sides on Vietnam*, edited by Cecil Woolf and John Bagguley, is a collection of essays by 168 well-known authors throughout the world. *Where is Vietnam?*, edited by Walter Lowenfels, consists of 92 poems about the war.

Many writers were publishing works for and against the war, but the genre that had the most impact was rock and folk music. Bob Dylan is an example of the musicians of the time. His music represented the hippie aesthetic and brilliant, swirling colors and hallucinogenic imagery. Some other bands that originated during this time and became well known for their psychedelic music, primarily about the Vietnam War in the early years, are the Grateful Dead, Jefferson Airplane, Big Brother, and Sly and the Family Stone. In England, the movement attracted the Beatles and the Rolling Stones.

Immigration

John Steinbeck's *Cannery Row* and *Tortilla Flats* glorify the lives of Mexican migrants in California. Amy Tan's *The Joy Luck Club* deals with the problems faced by Chinese immigrants. Leon Uris' *Exodus* deals with the social history that led to the founding of the modern state of Israel. It was published in 1958, only a short time after the Holocaust. It also deals with attempts of concentration camp survivors to get to the land that has become the nation of Israel. In many ways, it is the quintessential work on immigration—dealing with its causes and effects.

BRITISH LITERATURE

The Elizabethan Era

The reign of Elizabeth I ushered in a renaissance that led to the end of the medieval age. It was a very fertile literary period. The exploration of the New World expanded the vision of all levels of the social order from royalty to peasant, This was also the period when many rejected Catholicism in favor of a Christianity of their own. This era opened up new vistas to thought and daily life.

The manufacturing of cloth during this period increased, driving many people from the countryside into the cities. The population of London exploded, creating a metropolitan business center. William Caxton brought printing to England in the 1470s, and literacy increased from 30 percent in the fifteenth century to over 60 percent by 1530.

The Italian renaissance had a great influence on the renaissance in England. Early in the sixteenth century most written works were in Latin. It was assumed that a learned person must express his or her thoughts in that language. However, determination that vernacular English was valuable in writing emerged during this period. Queen Elizabeth's tutor Roger Ascham, for example, wrote in English.

In 1517 Luther's thesis, which brought on the *Reformation*—an attempt to return to pure Christianity—brought on the breakup of Western Christendom and eventually the secularization of society and the establishment of the king or queen as the head of this new/old church. It also brought about a new feeling that being religious was also being patriotic; it promoted nationalism.

The ascension of Elizabeth to the throne followed a very turbulent period regarding succession. She ruled for 45 peaceful years, which allowed arts and literature to flourish. Although she herself was headstrong and difficult, she had very shrewd political instincts and entrusted power to solid, talented men, most particularly Cecil, her Secretary, and Walsingham, whom she put in charge of foreign policy. She identified with her country as no previous ruler had and that in itself brought on a period of intense nationalism. She was a symbol of Englishness. The defeat of the Spanish Armada in 1588 was the direct result of the strong support she had from her own nation.

Drama was the principal form of literature in this age. Religious plays had been a part of the life of England for a long time, particularly the courtly life. However, in the Elizabethan age they became more and more secular and were created primarily for courtly entertainment. By the 1560s, Latin drama, particularly the tragedies of Seneca and the comedies of Plautus and Terence, began to wield an influence in England. Courtyards of inns became favorite places for the presentation of plays; but in 1576 the Earl of Leicester's men constructed their own building outside the city and called it The Theatre. Other theatres followed. Each had its own repertory company, and performances were given for profit but also for the queen and her court.

It is said that Shakespeare wrote *The Merry Wives of Windsor* at the specific command of the queen, who liked Falstaff and wanted to see him in love. It was also for the courtly audience that poetry was introduced into drama.

Shakespeare and Marlowe dominated the 1580s and 1590s and at the turn of the century, only a few years before Elizabeth's death, Ben Johnson began writing his series of satirical comedies.

Court favor was notoriously precarious and depended on the whims of the queen and others. Much of the satire of the period reflects the disappointment of writers like Edmund Spenser and John Lyly and the superficiality and treachery of the court atmosphere. "A thousand hopes, but all nothing," wrote Lyly, "a hundred promises, but yet nothing."

Not all literature was dictated by the court. The middle classes were developing and had their own style. Thomas Heywood and Thomas Deloney catered to bourgeois tastes.

The two universities of this period were also sources for the production of literature. The primary aim of the colleges was to develop ministers because there was a shortage brought on by the break with the Catholic Church. However, most university men couldn't make livings as ministers or academics, so they wrote as a way of earning income. Nashe, Marlowe, Robert Greene, and George Peele all reveal in their writings how difficult this path was.

Remuneration came mostly from patrons. Greene had sixteen different patrons from seventeen books whereas Shakespeare had a satisfactory relationship with the Earl of Southampton and didn't need to seek other support. Publishers would also sometimes pay for a manuscript, which they would then own. Unfortunately, if the manuscript did not pass muster with all who could condemn it—the court, the religious leaders, and prominent citizens—it was the author who was on the hot seat. Very few became as comfortable as Shakespeare did. His success came not only from his writing but also from his business acumen.

Writing was seen more as a craft than as an art in this period. There was not great conflict between art and nature and little distinction among literature, sports of the field, and the arts of the kitchen.

Balance and control were important in the England of this day, and this is reflected in the writing, especially in poetry. The *sestina*, a form in which the last words of each line in the first stanza are repeated in a different order in each of the following stanzas, became very popular. Verse forms ranged from the extremely simple four-line ballad stanza to the rather complicated form of the sonnet to the elaborate and beautiful eighteen-line stanza of Spenser's *Epithalamion*. Sonnets were called "quatorzains." The term "sonnet" was used loosely for any short poem. *Quatorzains* are fourteen-line poems in iambic pentameter with elaborate rhyme schemes.

However, Chaucer's seven-line rhyme royal stanza also survived in the sixteenth century. Shakespeare used it in *The Rape of Lucrece*, for example. An innovation was Spenser's nine-line stanza, called the Spenserian stanza, as used in *The Faerie Queene.*

As to themes, some of the darkness of the previous period can still be seen in some Elizabethan literature; for example, Shakespeare's *Richard II* (III.ii152–70). At the same time, a spirit of joy, gaiety, innocence, and lightheartedness can be seen in much of the most popular literature, and pastoral themes became popular. The theme of the burning desire for conquest and achievement was also significant in Elizabethan thought.

Some important writers of the Elizabethan age:

- Sir Thomas More (1478–1535)
- Sir Thomas Wyatt the Elder (1503–1542)
- Sir Philip Sidney (1554–1586)
- Edmund Spenser (1552–1599)
- Sir Walter Raleigh (1552–1618)
- John Lyly (1554–1606)
- George Peele (1556–1596)
- Christopher Marlowe (1564–1593)
- William Shakespeare (1564–1616)

The Victorian Age

The Victorian Age was a time of rapid change. Much of it was brought about by the **Industrial Revolution.** In England, the Industrial Revolution began with the development of the steam engine. However, the steam engine was only one component of the major technological, socioeconomic, and cultural innovations of the early nineteenth century that began in Britain and spread throughout the world. An economy based on manual labor was replaced by one dominated by industry and the manufacture of machinery. The textile industries also underwent very rapid growth and change. Canals were being built, roads were improving, and railways were being constructed.

The date of the Industrial Revolution varies according to how it is viewed. Some say that it began in the 1780s and wasn't fully perceived until the 1830s or 1840s. Others maintain that the beginning was earlier, about 1760, and began to manifest visible changes by 1830. The effects spread through Western Europe and North America throughout the nineteenth century, eventually affecting all major countries of the world. The impact on society has been compared to the period when agriculture began to develop and the nomadic lifestyle was abandoned.

The first Industrial Revolution was followed immediately by the Second Industrial Revolution around 1850 when the progress in technology and world economy gained momentum with the introduction of steam-powered ships and railways and eventually the internal combustion engine and electrical power generation.

The greatest sociological impact of the Industrial Revolution was the development of a middle class of industrialists and businessmen and the decline of the landed class of nobility and gentry. While working people had more opportunities for employment in the new mills and factories, working conditions were often less than desirable. Exploiting children for labor wasn't new, it was more apparent and perhaps more egregious as the need for cheap labor increased. In England, laws regarding employment of children began to be developed in 1833. Another effect of industrialization was the enormous shift from hand-produced goods to machine-produced ones and the resulting loss of jobs among weavers and others, which resulted in violence against the factories and machinery beginning in about 1811. Eventually the British government took measures to protect industry.

Another effect of the Industrial Revolution was the organization of labor. Because laborers were now working together in factories, mines, and mills, they were better able to organize to gain the advantages they felt they deserved. Conditions were bad enough in these workplaces that the energy to bring about change was significant and eventually trade unions emerged. Laborers quickly learned to use the weapon of the strike to get what they wanted. The strikes were often violent, and while the managers usually gave in to most of the demands made by strikers, animosity between management and labor was endemic.

The mass migration of rural families into urban areas also resulted in poor living conditions, long work hours, extensive use of children for labor, and a polluted atmosphere.

Another effect of industrialization of society was the separation of husband and wife. One person stayed at home and looked after the home and family and the other went off to work, a very different configuration than an agriculture-based economy where the entire family was usually involved in making a living. Gender roles began to be defined by the new configuration of labor in this new world order.

The application of industrial processes to printing brought about a great expansion in newspaper and popular book publishing. This, in turn, was followed by rapid increases in literacy and eventually in demands for mass political participation.

Romanticism, the literary, intellectual, and artistic movement that occurred along with the Industrial Movement, was actually a response to the increasing mechanization of society, an artistic hostility to what was taking over the world. Romanticism stressed the importance of nature in art and language in contrast to the monstrous machines and factories. Blake called them the "dark, satanic mills" in his poem, "And Did Those Feet in Ancient Time."

This movement followed on the heels of the **Enlightenment** period and was, at least in part, a reaction to the aristocratic and political norms of the previous period. Romanticism is sometimes called the *Counter-Enlightenment*. It stressed strong emotion, made individual imagination the critical authority, and overturned previous social conventions. Nature was important to the Romanticists and it elevated the achievements of misunderstood heroic individuals and artists who participated in altering society.

Some important Romantic writers:

- Johann Wolfgang von Goethe
- Walter Scott
- Ludwig Tieck
- E. T. A. Hoffman
- William Wordsworth
- Samuel Taylor Coleridge
- William Blake
- Victor Hugo
- Alexander Pushkin
- Lord Byron
- Washington Irving
- James Fenimore Cooper
- Henry Wadsworth Longfellow
- Edgar Allen Poe
- Emily Dickinson
- John Keats
- Percy Bysshe Shelley

Early Twentieth Century

World War I, also known as The First World War, the Great War, and The War to End All Wars, raged from July 1914 to the final Armistice on November 11, 1918. It was a world conflict between the Allied Powers led by Great Britain, France, Russia, and the United States (after 1917) and the Central Powers, led by the German Empire, the Austro-Hungarian Empire, and the Ottoman Empire. It brought down four great empires: The Austro-Hungarian, German, Ottoman, and Russian. It reconfigured European and Middle Eastern maps.

More than nine million soldiers died on the various battlefields and nearly that many more in the participating countries' home fronts, due to food shortages and genocide committed under the cover of various civil wars and internal conflicts.

However, more people died of the worldwide influenza outbreak at the end of the war and shortly after than died in the hostilities. The unsanitary conditions engendered by the war, severe overcrowding in barracks, wartime propaganda that interfered with public health warnings, and migration of so many soldiers around the world caused the influenza outbreak to become a pandemic.

The experiences of the war led to a sort of collective national trauma afterwards for all the participating countries. The optimism of the 1900s was entirely gone and those who fought in the war became what is known as "the Lost Generation" because they never fully recovered from their experiences. For the next few years memorials continued to be erected in thousands of European villages and towns.

A sense of disillusionment and cynicism is pronounced in literature and art from this period, and nihilism became popular. The world had never before witnessed such devastation, and its depiction in newspapers and on movie screens made the horrors more personal. War has always spawned bursts of creativity, and this war was no exception. Poetry, stories, and movies proliferated. In fact, World War I is still a fertile subject for art of all kinds, particularly literature and movies. In 2006, a young director by the name of Paul Gross created, directed, and starred in *Passchendaele*, which was based on his grandfather's stories, who was haunted all his life after killing a young German soldier in this War to End All Wars.

Some literature based on World War I:

- ⊙ "The Soldier," poem by Rupert Brooke
- ⊙ *Goodbye to All That*, autobiography by Robert Graves
- ⊙ "Anthem for Doomed Youth" and "Strange Meeting," poems by Wilfred Owen, published posthumously by Siegfried Sassoon in 1918
- ⊙ "In Flanders Fields," poem by John McCrae
- ⊙ *Three Soldiers,* novel by John Dos Passos
- ⊙ *Journey's End*, play by R. C. Sherriff
- ⊙ *All Quiet on the Western Front*, novel by Erich Maria Remarque
- ⊙ *Death of a Hero*, novel by Richard Aldington
- ⊙ *A Farewell to Arms*, novel by Ernest Hemingway
- ⊙ *Memoirs of an Infantry Officer*, novel by Siegfried Sassoon
- ⊙ *Sergeant York*, movie directed by Howard Hawks
- ⊙ The poetry of Wilfred Owen

World War II and Postcolonialism

The dissolution of the British Empire, the most extensive empire in world history and for a time the foremost global power, began in 1867 with its transformation into the modern Commonwealth. Dominion status was granted to the self-governing colonies of Canada in 1867, Australia in 1902, New Zealand in 1907, Newfoundland in 1907, and the newly created Union of South Africa in 1910.

Although the Allies won World War I and Britain's rule expanded into new areas, the heavy costs of the war made it less and less feasible to maintain the vast empire. Economic losses as well as human losses put increasing pressure on the Empire to give up its far-flung imperial posts in Asia and the African colonies. At the same time, nationalist sentiment was growing in both old and new Imperial territories fueled partly by their troops' contributions to the war and the anger of many non-white ex-servicemen at the racial discrimination they had encountered during their service.

The rise of anti-colonial nationalist movements in the subject territories and the changing economic situation of the world in the first half of the twentieth century challenged an imperial power now increasingly preoccupied with issues nearer home.

The Empire's end began with the onset of the Second World War when a deal was reached between the British government and the Indian independence movement whereby India would cooperate and remain loyal during the war but after which it would be granted independence. Following India's lead, nearly all of the other colonies would become independent over the next two decades.

Some literature based on World War II:

- ⊙ *Hiroshima* by John Hersey
- ⊙ *Cain Mutiny* Herman Wouk
- ⊙ *Catch 22* by Joseph Heller
- ⊙ *Slaughterhouse Five* by Kurt Vonnegut
- ⊙ *Summer of My German Soldier* by Bette Green
- ⊙ *Anne Frank—the Diary of a Young Girl*
- ⊙ *Night* by Elie Weisel

In the Caribbean, Africa, Asia, and the Pacific, post-war decolonization was achieved with haste in the face of increasingly powerful nationalist movements and Britain rarely fought to retain any territory.

Some representative literature:

- ⊙ *Heart of Darkness,* novel by Joseph Conrad
- ⊙ *Passage to India*, novel by E. M. Forster
- ⊙ "Gunga Din," poem by Rudyard Kipling

Ancient Literature

Between 7000 BCE and 3000 BCE critical events occurred that not only led to the invention of writing, thus making possible the emergence of literature, but also to the development of human civilization. These critical events included the domestication of animals, the development of agriculture, and the establishment of an agricultural surplus.

These three events allowed the small, nomadic groups of hunters and gathers who had previously existed in pockets all over the world to evolve into larger, stationary communities. The first of these communities to develop was in an area in the Middle East called Mesopotamia, meaning "Land Between two Rivers," the two rivers being the Tigris and the Euphrates. This early civilization was called Sumer and the people who lived there, who created the wheel and the first written language, were the **Sumerians**.

Perhaps the reason the Sumerians were the first to create so much of what is fundamental to civilization goes back to their unsurpassed ability to create an agricultural surplus. With their position between two rivers, the Sumerians developed an extensive irrigation system, which allowed them to create an abundant surplus. This surplus meant greater economic stability, security, and the ability to support a much larger population within the walls of their cities.

Hand in hand with a growing population was the need for governance and specialization. Artisans, governors, builders, regulators, and merchants were needed, as well as priests and temples for the flourishing religion. Keeping track of all this activity required the development of some kind of record keeping. At first, pictographs, or images directly representing concrete objects, were etched into soft clay tablets and allowed to dry.

As time went on, the demand on the record keepers grew from recording how many sacks of barley a farmer brought to the temple to describing, in great detail and enthusiasm, the exploits of the kings and gods. Thus, with the evolution of the city-state and then the nation, pictographs became insufficient to meet the needs of this increasingly complex civilization. Eventually the Sumerians developed symbols to represent not only concrete items such as corn and cattle, but also such abstract qualities as courage and love. Thus the precursor of modern writing began.

http://www.crystalinks.com/sumerart.html (for photo)

Skill 1.6   Recognizing various strategic approaches to and elements of teaching reading and textual interpretation

NONFICTION

The first question to ask when approaching a reading task is: What is my objective? What do I want to achieve from this reading? How will I use the information I gain from this reading? Do I only need to grasp the gist of the piece? Do I need to know the line of reasoning—not only the thesis but also the subpoints? Will I be reporting important and significant details orally or in a written document?

A written document can be expected to have a **thesis**—either expressed or derived. To discover the thesis, the reader needs to ask what point the writer intends to make. The writing can also be expected to be organized in some logical way and to have subpoints that support or establish that the thesis is valid. It is also reasonable to expect that there will be details or examples that will support the subpoints. Knowing this, the reader can make a decision about reading techniques required for the purpose.

If the reader only needs to know the gist of a written document, *scanning* techniques may be sufficient. To scan, using the forefinger, move the eyes down the page, picking up the important statements in each paragraph and deducing what the piece is about.

If the reader needs to get a better grasp of how the writer achieved hi or her purpose in the document, a quick and cursory glance—a *skimming*—of each paragraph will yield what the subpoints are, the topic sentences of the paragraphs, and how the thesis is developed, yielding a greater understanding of the author's purpose and method of development than a scan could give.

In-depth reading requires the careful scrutiny of each phrase and sentence, looking for the thesis first and then the topic sentences in the paragraphs that provide the development of the thesis. The reader must also look for connections such as transitional devices that provide clues to the direction the reasoning is taking.

Sometimes rereading is necessary in order to make use of a piece of writing for an oral or written report.

FICTION

To *interpret* means essentially to read with understanding and appreciation. It is not as daunting as it may sound. Simple techniques for interpreting literature are as follows:

- ⊙ **Context:** This includes the author's feelings, beliefs, past experiences, goals, needs, and physical environment. Incorporate an understanding of how these elements may have affected the writing to enrich an interpretation of it.
- ⊙ **Symbols:** Symbols can have personal, cultural, or universal associations. Use an understanding of symbols to unearth the theme or meaning the author might have intended but not expressed.
- ⊙ **Diction:** Examine the diction, exploring the unusual words, figurative language, sensory images, and sound devices.
- ⊙ **Questions:** Asking questions, such as "How would I react in this situation?" may shed further light on how you feel about the work.

READING EMPHASIS IN MIDDLE SCHOOL

Reading for comprehension of factual material—content-area textbooks, reference books, and newspapers—is closely related to study strategies in the middle or junior high school. Organized study models, such as the SQ3R (Survey, Question, Read, Recite, and Review) method, a technique that makes it possible to learn the content of even large amounts of text, teach students to locate main ideas and supporting details, to recognize sequential order, to distinguish fact from opinion, and to determine cause/effect relationships.

Strategies

1. Teacher-guided activities that require students to organize and to summarize information based on the author's explicit intent are pertinent strategies in middle grades. Evaluation techniques include oral and written responses to standardized or teacher-made worksheets.
2. Reading fiction introduces and reinforces skills in inferring meaning from narration and description. Guided reading and thinking activities can help students understand and analyze narrative texts. As teachers model their thinking processes students begin to understand how to gain deeper meaning from a text. Many printed reading-for-comprehension instruments as well as individualized computer software programs exist to monitor the progress of acquiring comprehension skills.
3. Older middle school students should be given opportunities for more student-centered activities—individual and collaborative selection of reading choices based on student interest, small group discussions of selected works, and greater written expression. Evaluation techniques include teacher monitoring and observation of discussions and written work samples.
4. Certain students may begin some fundamental critical interpretation—recognizing fallacious reasoning in news media, examining the accuracy of news reports and advertising, or explaining their reasons for preferring one author's writing to another's. Development of these skills may require a more learning-centered approach in which the teacher identifies a number of objectives and suggested resources from which the student may choose a course of study. Self-evaluation through a reading diary should be stressed. Teacher and peer evaluation of creative projects resulting from such study is encouraged.
5. Reading aloud before the entire class as a formal means of teacher evaluation should be phased out in favor of one-to-one tutoring or peer-assisted reading. Occasional sharing of favored selections by both teacher and willing students is a good oral interpretation basic.

READING EMPHASIS IN HIGH SCHOOL

Students in high school literature classes should focus on interpretive and critical reading. Teachers should guide the study of the elements of inferential (interpretive) reading—drawing conclusions, predicting outcomes, and recognizing examples of specific genre characteristics, for example—and critical reading to judge the quality of the writer's work against recognized standards.

At this level, students should understand the skills of language and reading that they are expected to master and be able to evaluate their own progress.

Strategies

1. The teacher becomes more facilitator than instructor—helping the student to make a diagnosis of his own strengths and weaknesses, keeping a record of progress, and interacting with other students and the teacher in practicing skills. Methods of controlled groups discussions, such as the **Socratic Seminar**, work well with high school students. The Socratic Seminar method of teaching is based on Socrates' theory that it is more important to enable students to think for themselves than to merely fill their heads with "right" answers. Students are given opportunities to closely examine a common text from a novel, poem, art print, or even a piece of music. After reading the text, open-ended questions are posed. Open-ended questions allow students to think critically, analyze multiple meanings in text, and express ideas with clarity and confidence. Dialogue is exploratory and students are required to suspend any biases and prejudices. Students in a Socratic Seminar respond to one another with respect by carefully listening instead of interrupting. Careful rules dictate behavior.

2. Despite the requisites and prerequisites of most literature courses, students should be encouraged to pursue independent study and enrichment reading.

3. Ample opportunities should be provided for oral interpretation of literature, for special projects in creative dramatics, writing for publication in school literary magazines or newspapers, and speech/debate activities. A student portfolio provides for teacher and peer evaluation.

4. Tracing an idea through a passage goes much better if a strategy is developed for doing so. Good readers usually have these strategies even though they might not be aware of them. A good way to start is by looking for motifs or repeated words or phrases. Following motifs will make it possible to observe a picture of the idea as it appears in the piece of writing.

5. Students should also be encouraged to look for transitional words in writing. Transitional words and phrases are designed to lead the reader forward and through a piece of writing. Such words as *therefore, however, even so, although*, etc. are clues to relationships. Phrases sometimes

substitute for words. Some examples are *as a matter of fact, in the long run, looking back*, etc.

6. Students should also be equipped with techniques for analyzing a text, for example, DIDLS (Diction, Imagery, Details, Language, Sentence Structure or Syntax), which is a prose analysis method. Students are taught to systematically look for each of these elements in a piece of prose, after which they are able to identify the tone of the writing.

7. Methods are available for poetry and also for expository texts. For example, the TPCASTT is a good method for poetry. Students analyze the Title, then Paraphrase the poem, look for Connotative meanings, identify the Attitude (tone), identify Shifts, examine the Title again, and finally identify the Theme.

Learning Approach

Early theories of language development were formulated from learning theory research. The assumption was that language development evolved from learning the rules of language structures and applying them through imitation and reinforcement. This approach also assumed that language, cognitive, and social developments were independent of each other. Thus, children were expected to learn language from patterning after adults who spoke and wrote Standard English. No allowance was made for communication through child jargon, idiomatic expressions, or grammatical and mechanical errors resulting from overly strict adherence to the rules of inflection (*childs* instead of *children*) or conjugation (*runned* instead of *ran*). No association was made between physical and operational development and language mastery.

Linguistic Approach

Studies spearheaded by Noam Chomsky in the 1950s formulated the theory that language ability is innate and develops through natural human maturation as environmental stimuli trigger acquisition of syntactical structures appropriate to each exposure level. The assumption of a hierarchy of syntax downplayed the significance of semantics. Because of the complexity of syntax and the relative speed with which children acquire language, linguists attributed language development to biological rather than cognitive or social influences.

Cognitive Approach

Researchers in the 1970s proposed that language knowledge derives from both syntactic and semantic structures. Drawing on the studies of Piaget and other cognitive learning theorists (see Skill 4.7), supporters of the cognitive approach maintained that children acquire knowledge of linguistic structures after they have acquired the cognitive structures necessary to process language. For example, joining words for specific meaning necessitates sensory motor intelligence. The child must be able to coordinate movement and recognize objects before he or she can identify words to name the objects or word groups to describe the actions performed with those objects.

Adolescents must have developed the mental abilities for *organizing concepts as well as concrete operations, predicting outcomes,* and *theorizing* before they can assimilate and verbalize complex sentence structures, choose vocabulary for particular nuances of meaning, and examine semantic structures for tone and manipulative effect.

Socio-cognitive Approach

Other theorists in the 1970s proposed that language development results from sociolinguistic competence. Language, cognitive, and social knowledge are interactive elements of total human development. Emphasis on verbal communication as the medium for language expression resulted in the inclusion of speech activities in most language arts curricula.

Unlike previous approaches, the socio-cognitive approach believes that determining the appropriateness of language in given situations for specific listeners is as important as understanding semantic and syntactic structures. By engaging in conversation, children at all stages of development have opportunities to test their language skills, receive feedback, and make modifications. As a social activity, conversation is as structured by social order as grammar is structured by the rules of syntax. Conversation satisfies the learner's need to be heard and understood and to influence others. Thus, his choices of vocabulary, tone, and content are dictated by his ability to assess the language knowledge of his listeners. He is constantly applying his cognitive skills to using language in a social interaction. If the capacity to acquire language is inborn, without an environment in which to practice language a child would not pass beyond the grunts and gestures of primitive man.

Of course, the varying degrees of environmental stimuli to which children are exposed at all age levels affects the speed of language development . Some children are prepared to articulate concepts and recognize symbolism by the time they enter fifth grade because they have been exposed to challenging reading and conversations with well-spoken adults at home or in their social groups. Others are still trying to master the sight recognition skills and are not yet ready to combine words in complex patterns.

Concerns for the Teacher

Because teachers must, by virtue of tradition and the dictates of the curriculum, teach grammar, usage, and writing as well as reading and, later, literature, the problem becomes when to teach what to whom. The profusion of approaches to teaching grammar alone are mind-boggling. At a university level we learn about transformational grammar, stratification grammar, sectoral grammar, etc. But in practice, most teachers, supported by presentations in textbooks and by the methods they have learned themselves, keep coming back to the same traditional prescriptive approach (read and imitate) or structural approach (learn the parts of speech, the parts of a sentence, punctuation rules, and sentence patterns). For some educators, the best solution is the worst—not teaching grammar at all.

Problems also occur in teaching usage. One question that is difficult to answer is: Do we require students to communicate strictly in Standard English? Different schools of thought suggest that a study of dialect and idiom and a recognition of various jargons is a vital part of language development. Social pressures, especially on students in middle and junior high schools, to be accepted within their peer groups and to speak the nonstandard language spoken outside the school make adolescents resistant to the corrective, remedial approach. In many communities where the immigrant populations are high, new words are entering English from other languages even as words and expressions that were common when we were children have become rare or obsolete.

Regardless of differences of opinion concerning language development, it is safe to say that a language arts teacher will be most effective using the styles and approaches with which she is most comfortable. And, if she subscribes to a student-centered approach, she may find that the students have a lot to teach her and each other. Moffett and Wagner, in the Fourth Edition of *Student-centered Language Arts K–12*, stress the three *I*s: individualization, interaction, and integration. Essentially, they are supporting the socio-cognitive approach to language development. By providing an opportunity for the student to select his own activities and resources, his instruction is individualized. By centering on and teaching each other, students are interactive. Finally, by allowing students to synthesize a variety of knowledge structures, they integrate them. The teacher's role becomes that of a facilitator.

Benefits of the Socio-cognitive Approach

Most basal readers utilize an integrated, cross-curricular approach to successful grammar, language, and usage. Reinforcement becomes an intradepartmental responsibility. Language incorporates diction and terminology across the curriculum. Standard usage is encouraged and supported by both the core classroom textbooks and current software for technology. Teachers need to acquaint themselves with the computer capabilities in their school district and at their individual school sites. Advances in new technologies require the teacher to familiarize herself with programs that would serve her students' needs. Students respond enthusiastically to technology. Several highly effective programs are available in various formats to assist students with initial instruction or remediation. Grammar texts, such as the Warriner's series, employ various methods to reach individual learning styles. The school library media center should become a focal point for individual exploration.

ENGLISH LANGUAGE LEARNERS

Students who are raised in homes where English is not the first language and/or where standard English is not spoken may have difficulty with hearing the difference between similar sounding words like "send" and "sent."

Any student who is not in an environment where English phonology operates may have difficulty perceiving and demonstrating the differences between English language phonemes. If students cannot hear the difference between words that sound the same, like "grow" and "glow," they will be confused when these words appear in a print context. This confusion will impact their comprehension.

Considerations for teaching to English Language Learners include recognition by the teacher that what works for the English language speaking student from an English language speaking family does not necessarily work in other languages.

Research recommends that ELL students initially learn to read in their first language. It has been found that a priority for ELL should be learning to speak English before being learning to read English because speaking lays the foundation for phonological awareness.

Children who learn to read on schedule and who are avid readers have been seen to have superior vocabularies compared to other children their age. The reason for this is that in order to understand what they read they must often determine the meaning for a word based on its context. Children who constantly turn to a dictionary for the meaning of a word they don't know will not have this advantage.

This is an important clue for providing students the kinds of exercises and help they need in order to develop their vocabularies. Learning vocabulary lists is useful, of course, but much less efficient than exercises for determining meaning on the basis of context. Determining meaning based on context requires an entirely different kind of thinking and learning than memorizing lists does.

Poetry—especially rhymed poetry—is also useful for developing vocabulary exercises for children, because the pronunciation of a term may be deduced by what the poet intended for it to rhyme with. In some poets of earlier periods, the teacher may need to intervene because some of the words that would have rhymed when the poem was written do not rhyme in today's English. Even so, this is a good opportunity to help children understand some of the important principles of their constantly changing language.

Another good exercise for developing vocabulary is the crossword puzzle. A child's ability to think in terms of analogy is a step toward mature language understanding and use. The teacher may construct crossword puzzles using items from the class such as students' names or the terms from their literature or language lessons.

COMPETENCY 2.0 LANGUAGE AND LINGUISTICS

GRAMMAR AND MECHANICS EXPECTATIONS ON A COMPETENCY EXAM

The candidate should be cognizant of proper rules and conventions of punctuation, capitalization, and spelling. Competency exams will generally test the ability to apply the more advanced skills; thus, a limited number of more frustrating rules are presented here. On any exam, rules should be applied according to the American style of English, i.e., spelling *theater* instead of *theatre* and placing terminal marks of punctuation almost exclusively within other marks of punctuation.

Skill 2.1 Understanding elements of traditional grammar

SENTENCE COMPLETENESS

Avoid fragments and run-on sentences. The recognition of sentence elements necessary to make a complete thought, proper use of independent and dependent clauses (see *Use correct coordination and subordination*), and proper punctuation will correct sentence errors.

SENTENCE STRUCTURE

Recognize simple, compound, complex, and compound-complex sentences. Use dependent (subordinate) and independent clauses correctly to create these sentence structures.

Simple	Joyce wrote a letter.
Compound	Joyce wrote a letter and Dot drew a picture.
Complex	While Joyce wrote a letter Dot drew a picture.
Compound/Complex	When Mother asked the girls to demonstrate their new-found skills, Joyce wrote a letter and Dot drew a picture.

Note: Do **not** confuse compound sentence elements with compound sentences.

Simple sentence with compound subject:

> *Joyce* and *Dot* wrote letters.
> The *girl* in row three and the *boy* next to her were passing notes across the aisle.

Simple sentence with compound predicate:

> *Joyce wrote letters and drew pictures.*

The captain of the high school debate team <u>graduated with honors</u> and <u>studied broadcast journalism in college</u>.

Simple sentence with compound object of preposition:

Colleen graded the students' essays for <u>style</u> and <u>mechanical accuracy</u>.

Parallelism

Recognize parallel structures using phrases (prepositional, gerund, participial, and infinitive) and omissions from sentences that create the lack of parallelism.

Prepositional phrase/single modifier

Incorrect: *Colleen ate the ice cream with enthusiasm and hurriedly.*
Correct: *Colleen ate the ice cream with enthusiasm and speed.*
Correct: *Colleen ate the ice cream enthusiastically and hurriedly.*

Participial phrase/infinitive phrase

Incorrect: *After hiking for hours and to sweat profusely, Joe sat down to rest and drinking water.*
Correct: *After hiking for hours and sweating profusely, Joe sat down to rest and drink water*

Syntactical Redundancy or Omission

Errors in redundancy or omission occur when superfluous words have been added to a sentence or when key words have been omitted from a sentence.

Redundancy

Incorrect: *Joyce made sure that when her plane arrived that she retrieved all of her luggage.*
Correct: *Joyce made sure that when her plane arrived she retrieved all of her luggage.*

Incorrect: *He was a mere skeleton of his former self.*
Correct: *He was a skeleton of his former self.*

Omission

Incorrect: *Dot opened her book, recited her textbook, and answered the teacher's subsequent question.*
Correct: *Dot opened her book, recited from her textbook, and answered the teacher's subsequent question.*

Double Negatives

Eliminate double negatives. Using a double negative occurs when positioning two negatives that, in fact, cancel each other in meaning.

> Incorrect: *Dot didn't have no double negatives in her paper.*
> Correct: *Dot didn't have any double negatives in her paper.*

TYPES OF CLAUSES

Clauses are connected word groups that are composed of *at least* one subject and one verb. (The subject is the part about which something is being said. The verb either conveys action or links the subject.)

> <u>Students</u> are <u>waiting</u> for the start of the assembly.
> Subject   Verb

> At the end of the play, <u>students</u> <u>wait</u> for the curtain to come down.
>   Subject Verb

Clauses can be **independent** or **dependent**.

Independent clauses can stand alone or they can be joined to other clauses using conjunctions such as *for, and, nor, but, or, yet*, and *so*.

The structure of a sentence using independent or dependent clauses will be one of the following:

Independent clause	,	Independent clause
Dependent clause	,	Independent clause
Independent clause		Dependent clause

Dependent clauses, by definition, contain at least one subject and one verb. However, they cannot stand alone as complete sentences. They are structurally dependent on the main clause.

There are two types of dependent clauses: (1) those with a subordinating conjunction, and (2) those with a relative pronoun.

Sample **coordinating conjunctions**:

- ⊙ Although
- ⊙ When
- ⊙ If
- ⊙ Unless
- ⊙ Because

Unless a cure is discovered, many more people will die of the disease.
dependent clause   +   independent clause

Sample **relative pronouns**:

- ⊙ Who
- ⊙ Whom
- ⊙ Which
- ⊙ That

The White House has an official website, which contains press releases, news updates, and biographies of the president and vice president.
(independent clause + relative pronoun + relative dependent clause)

MISPLACED AND DANGLING MODIFIERS

Particular phrases that are not placed near the word they modify often result in **misplaced modifiers**. Particular phrases that do not relate to the subject being modified result in **dangling modifiers**.

Misplaced modifiers create confusion.

Misplaced modifier: *Sally discovered a charming old bookstore wandering through the busy streets.*
Correct: *Wandering through the busy streets, Sally discovered a charming old bookstore.*

Dangling modifiers create ambiguity and unintended meaning. The problem with a sentence containing a dangling modifier is that the person or thing being modified is not included in the sentence.

Dangling modifier: *Relaxing in the bathtub, the telephone rang.*
Correct: *While I was relaxing in the bathtub, the telephone rang.*

Dangling modifier: *After watching the documentary, the issue was still not clear.*
Correct: *After watching the documentary, I still did not understand the issue.*

SPELLING

This section will concentrate on spelling plurals and possessives.

The multiplicity and complexity of spelling rules based on phonics, letter doubling, and exceptions to rules—which have not been mastered by adulthood—should be replaced by a good dictionary and spell check. Because spelling mastery is also difficult for adolescents, our recommendation is the same. Learning the use of a dictionary and thesaurus will be a more rewarding use of time than memorization of extensive lists of rules and exceptions.

Most plurals of nouns that end in hard consonants or hard consonant sounds followed by a silent *e* are made by adding *s*. Some words ending in vowels only add *s*.

fingers, numerals, banks, bugs, riots, homes, gates, radios, bananas

Nouns that end in soft the consonant sounds *s*, *j*, *x*, *z*, *ch*, and *sh* add *es*. Some nouns ending in *o* add *es*.

dresses, waxes, churches, brushes, tomatoes, potatoes

Nouns ending in *y* preceded by a vowel just add *s*.

boys, alleys

Nouns ending in *y* preceded by a consonant change the *y* to *i* and add *es*.

babies, corollaries, frugalities, poppies

Some noun plurals are formed irregularly or remain the same as the singular forms.

sheep, deer, children, leaves, oxen

Some nouns derived from foreign words, especially Latin, may make their plurals in two different ways, one of them Anglicized. Sometimes the meanings are the same; other times, the two plurals are used in slightly different contexts. It is always wise to consult the dictionary in these cases.

appendices, appendixes
criterion, criteria
indexes, indices
crisis, crises

Make the plurals of closed (solid) compound words in the usual way except for words ending in *–ful*, which make their plurals on the root word.

timelines, hairpins, cupsful

Make the plurals of open or hyphenated compounds by adding the change in inflection to the word that changes in number.

fathers-in-law, courts-martial, masters of art, doctors of medicine

Make the plurals of letters, numbers, and abbreviations by adding *s.*

*fives and tens, IBMs, 1990s, p*s *and q*s (Note that letters are italicized.)

CAPITALIZATION

Capitalize all proper names of persons (including specific organizations or agencies of government); places (countries, states, cities, parks, and specific geographical areas); things (political parties, structures, historical and cultural terms, and calendar and time designations); and religious terms (any deity, revered person or group, and sacred writings).

Percy Bysshe Shelley, Argentina, Mount Rainier National Park, Grand Canyon, League of Nations, the Sears Tower, Birmingham, Lyric Theater, Americans, Midwesterners, Democrats, Renaissance, Boy Scouts of America, Easter, God, Bible, Dead Sea Scrolls, Koran

Capitalize proper adjectives and titles used with proper names.

California gold rush, President John Adams, French fries, Homeric epic, Romanesque architecture, Senator John Glenn

Note: Some words that represent titles and offices are not capitalized unless used with a proper name.

Capitalized	Not Capitalized
Congressman McKay	the congressman from Florida
Commander Alger	commander of the Pacific Fleet
Queen Elizabeth	the queen of England

Capitalize all main words in titles of works of literature, art, and music. (See "Using Italics" in the Punctuation section.)

PUNCTUATION

Using Terminal Punctuation in Relation to Quotation Marks

In a quoted statement that is either declarative or imperative, place the period inside the closing quotation marks.

"The airplane crashed on the runway during takeoff."

If the quotation is followed by other words in the sentence, place a comma inside the closing quotation marks and a period at the end of the sentence.

> *"The airplane crashed on the runway during takeoff," said the announcer.*

In most instances in which a quoted title or expression occurs at the end of a sentence, the period is placed before either the single or double quotation marks.

> *"The middle-school readers were unprepared to understand Bryant's poem 'Thanatopsis.'"*
> *Early book-length adventure stories like* Don Quixote *and* The Three Musketeers *were known as "picaresque novels."*

There is an instance in which the final quotation mark would precede the period. If the content of the sentence is about a speech or quote so that the understanding of the meaning would be confused by the placement of the period, place the period outside the quotation marks.

> *The first thing out of his mouth was "Hi, I'm home".*
> *The first line of his speech began "I arrived home to an empty house".*

In sentences that are interrogatory or exclamatory, the question mark or exclamation point should be positioned outside the closing quotation marks if the quote itself is a statement, a command, or a cited title.

> *Who decided to lead us in the recitation of the "Pledge of Allegiance"?*
> *Why was Tillie shaking as she began her recitation, "Once upon a midnight dreary . . ."?*
> *I was embarrassed when Mrs. White said, "Your slip is showing"!*

In sentences that are declarative but the quotation is a question or an exclamation, place the question mark or exclamation point inside the quotation marks.

> *The hall monitor yelled, "Fire! Fire!"*
> *"Fire! Fire!" yelled the hall monitor.*
> *Cory shrieked, "Is there a mouse in the room?"* (In this instance, the question supersedes the exclamation.)

Using Periods with Parentheses or Brackets

Place the period inside the parentheses or brackets if they enclose a complete sentence, independent of the other sentences around it.

Stephen Crane was a confirmed alcohol and drug addict. (He admitted as much to other journalists in Cuba.)

If the parenthetical expression is a statement inserted within another statement, the period in the enclosure is omitted.

Mark Twain used the character Indian Joe (he also appeared in The Adventures of Tom Sawyer*) as a foil for Jim in* The Adventures of Huckleberry Finn.

When enclosed matter comes at the end of a sentence requiring quotation marks, place the period outside the parentheses or brackets.

"The secretary of state consulted with the ambassador [Albright]."

Using Commas

Separate two or more coordinate adjectives that modify the same word and three or more nouns, phrases, or clauses in a list.

Maggie's hair was dull, dirty, and lice-ridden.

Dickens portrayed the Artful Dodger as skillful pickpocket, loyal follower of Fagin, and defendant of Oliver Twist.

Ellen daydreamed about getting out of the rain, taking a shower, and eating a hot dinner.

In Elizabethan England, Ben Johnson wrote comedies, Christopher Marlowe wrote tragedies, and William Shakespeare composed both.

Use commas to separate antithetical or complimentary expressions from the rest of the sentence.

The veterinarian, not his assistant, would perform the delicate surgery.

The more he knew about her, the less he wished he knew.

Randy hopes to, and probably will, get an appointment to the Naval Academy.

His thorough, though esoteric, scientific research could not easily be understood by high school students.

Using Double Quotation Marks with Other Punctuation

Quotations—whether words, phrases, or clauses—should be punctuated according to the rules of the grammatical function they serve in the sentence.

The works of Shakespeare, "the Bard of Avon," have been contested as originating with other authors.

"You'll get my money," the old man warned, "when 'Hell freezes over'."

Sheila cited the passage that began "Four score and seven years ago...." (Note the ellipsis followed by an enclosed period.)

"Old Ironsides" inspired the preservation of the U.S.S. Constitution.

Use quotation marks to enclose the titles of shorter works: songs, short poems, short stories, essays, and chapters of books. (See "Using Italics" for punctuating longer titles.)

"The Tell-Tale Heart"   "Casey at the Bat"   "America the Beautiful"

Using Semicolons

Use semicolons to separate independent clauses when the second clause is introduced by a transitional adverb. (These clauses may also be written as separate sentences, preferably by placing the adverb within the second sentence.)

The Elizabethans modified the rhyme scheme of the sonnet; thus, it was called the English sonnet.
or
The Elizabethans modified the rhyme scheme of the sonnet. It thus was called the English sonnet.

Use semicolons to separate items in a series that are long and complex or have internal punctuation.

The Italian Renaissance produced masters in the fine arts: Dante Alighieri, author of the Divine Comedy*; Leonardo da Vinci, painter of* The Last Supper*; and Donatello, sculptor of the* QuattroCoronati, *the four saints.*

The leading scorers in the WNBA were Haizhaw Zheng, averaging 23.9 points per game; Lisa Leslie, 22; and Cynthia Cooper, 19.5.

Using Colons

Place a colon at the beginning of a list of items. (Note its use in the sentence about Renaissance Italians in the paragraph above.)

> *The teacher directed us to compare Faulkner's three symbolic novels:* Absalom, Absalom, As I Lay Dying, *and* Light in August.

Do **not** use a comma if the list is preceded by a verb.

> *Three of Faulkner's symbolic novels are* Absalom, Absalom; As I Lay Dying, *and* Light in August.

Using Dashes

Place em dashes to denote sudden breaks in thought.

> *Some periods in literature—the Romantic Age, for example—spanned different time periods in different countries.*

Use em dashes instead of commas if commas are used elsewhere in the sentence for amplification or explanation.

> *The Fireside Poets included three Brahmans—James Russell Lowell, Henry David Wadsworth, and Oliver Wendell Holmes—and John Greenleaf Whittier.*

Using Italics

Use italics to punctuate the titles of long works of literature, names of periodical publications, musical scores, works of art, and television and radio programs. (When unable to write in italics, students should be instructed to underline in their own writing where italics would be appropriate.)

> *The Idylls of the King*   *Hiawatha*   *The Sound and the Fury*
> *Mary Poppins*   *Newsweek*   *The Nutcracker Suite*

IDENTIFICATION OF COMMON MORPHEMES, PREFIXES, AND SUFFIXES

This aspect of vocabulary development is to help students look for structural elements within words that can be used independently to help determine meaning.

The terms listed below are generally recognized as the key structural analysis components.

Root words: A root word is a word from which another word is developed. The second word can be said to have its "root" in the first.

Base words: A stand-alone linguistic unit that cannot be deconstructed or broken down into smaller words. For example, in the word "retell" the base word is "tell."

Contractions: These are shortened forms of two words in which a letter or letters have been deleted. These deleted letters have been replaced by an apostrophe.

Prefixes: These are beginning units of meaning added (the vocabulary word for this type of structural adding is *affixed*) to a base word or root word. They are also sometimes known as *bound morphemes*, meaning that they cannot stand alone as base words.

Suffixes: These are ending units of meaning affixed or added to the ends of root or base words. Suffixes transform the original meanings of base and root words. Like prefixes, they are also known as bound morphemes

Compound words: A compound word occurs when two or more base words are connected to form a new word. The meaning of the new word is in some way connected with that of the base words.

Inflectional endings: These are types are suffixes that impart a new meaning to the base or root word. These endings change the gender, number, tense, or form of the base or root words. Just like other suffixes, these are termed bound morphemes.

Skill 2.2   Understanding various semantic elements

Slang is language outside the conventional use and is informal in its vocabulary and idiomatic expressions. It is often more playful and more metaphorical than formal language, and it often first appears in the language of groups with low status. It is often taboo and unlikely to be used by people of high status and tends to displace conventional terms, either as a shorthand or as a defense against perceptions associated with the conventional terms.

Slang comes about for many reasons. Amelioration is one reason, which often results in euphemisms. (See Skill 1.3 Figurative Language)

Some slang has become so embedded in the language that its sources are long forgotten. For example, "fame" originally meant "rumor." Some words that were originally intended as euphemisms, such as "mentally retarded" and "moron" to avoid using the word "idiot," have themselves become pejorative.

Informal language and **formal language** are distinguished on the occasion as well as the audience. At a formal occasion—for example, of executives or of government officials—even conversational exchanges likely to be more formal. A cocktail party or a golf game are examples where language is likely to be informal. Formal language uses fewer or no contractions, less slang, longer sentences, and more organization in longer segments. It often contains elevated diction.

Jargon is the specialized vocabulary of a particular industry or profession, such as the computer industry, the teaching profession, and the law profession. It may also be the vocabulary of a social group. A speaker must be knowledgeable about and sensitive to his audience to know what jargon is appropriate to use.

Technical language is a form of jargon. It is usually specific to an industry, profession, or field of study.

Regionalisms are those usages that are specific to a particular part of the country. A good example is the second person plural pronoun: *you*. Because the plural is the same as the singular, various parts of the country have developed their own solutions to be sure that they are understood when they are speaking to more than one "you." In the South, "you-all" or "y'all" is common. In the Northeast, one often hears "youse." In some areas of the Midwest, "you'ns" can be heard.

Vocabulary also varies from region to region. A small stream is a "creek" in some regions but "crick" in others. In Boston, a soft drink is generically called a "tonic," but it becomes "soda" in other parts of the northeast. It is "liqueur" in Canada, and "pop" when you get west of New York.

SEMANTICS

To effectively teach language it is necessary to understand that as human beings acquire language they realize that words have **denotative** and **connotative** meanings. Generally, denotative words point to things and connotative words deal with mental suggestions that the words convey. The word *skunk* has a denotative meaning if the speaker can point to the actual animal as he speaks the word and intends the word to identify the animal. *Skunk* has connotative meaning depending upon the tone of delivery, the socially acceptable attitudes about the animal, and the speaker's personal feelings about the animal.

(See also Skill 1.3 Identifying and Analyzing Figurative Language and Other Literary Elements)

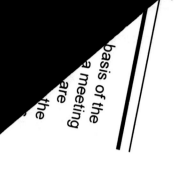

e definitions agreed upon by the society in which the
a black and white mammal of the weasel family with
h secrete a pungent odor." The *Merriam Webster*
. . and offensive" odor. Identification of the color,
acteristics are informative. The interpretation of the
e.

are the personal feelings a word arouses. A child who
has no p_____nce with a skunk and its odor or has had a pet skunk will
feel differently abou_ _ _ word *skunk* than a child who has smelled the spray or
been conditioned vicariously to associate offensiveness with the animal denoted
skunk. The very fact that our society views a skunk as an animal to be avoided will
affect the child's interpretation of the word. In fact, it is not necessary for one to
have actually seen a skunk (that is, have a denotative understanding) to use the
word in either connotative expression. For example, one child might call another
child a skunk, connoting an unpleasant reaction (affective use) or, seeing another
small black and white animal, call it a skunk based on the definition (informative
use).

Using Connotations

In everyday language we unconsciously attach affective meanings to words; we
exercise more conscious control of informative connotations. In the process of
language development, the leaner must not only grasp the definitions of words but
also grasp the affective connotations and how his listeners process these
connotations. Gaining this conscious control over language makes it possible to
use language appropriately in various situations and to evaluate its uses in
literature and other forms of communication.

The manipulation of language for a variety of purposes is the goal of language
instruction. Advertisers and satirists are especially conscious of the effect word
choice has on their audiences. By evoking the proper responses writers and
advertisements can convince readers and listeners to take action.

Choice of the medium through which the message is delivered is a significant
factor in controlling language. Spoken language relies as much on the gestures,
facial expressions, and tone of voice of the speaker as on the words he speaks.
Slapstick comics can evoke laughter without speaking a word. Young children use
body language overtly and older children use it more subtly to convey messages.
Working strictly with the written word, the writer must carefully choose the right
words to imply the body language, inflection, and emotion.

Teaching Tip: *One method for teaching the connotations of words is the Frayer Method of vocabulary instruction.*

The **Frayer Model** is a graphical organizer used for word analysis and vocabulary building. This four-square model asks students to think about and describe the meaning of a word or concept by first defining the term, then describing its essential characteristics, next providing examples of the idea, and then offering nonexamples of the idea.

Frayer Model

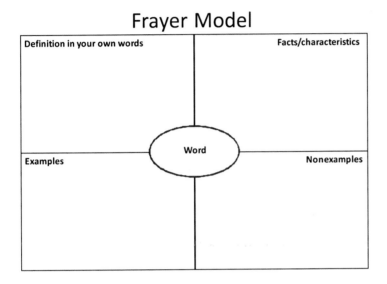

This strategy stresses understanding words within the larger context of a reading selection by requiring students to first analyze the items (definition and characteristics) and then to synthesize/apply this information by thinking of examples and nonexamples.

Skill 2.3 Understanding subjects relating to the analysis and history of English

English is an Indo-European language that evolved through several periods. The origin of English dates to the settlement of the British Isles in the fifth and sixth centuries CE by Germanic tribes called the Angles, Saxons, and Jutes. The original Britons spoke a Celtic tongue, while the Angles spoke a Germanic dialect. Modern English derives from the speech of the Anglo-Saxons who imposed not only their language but also their social customs and laws on their new land. From the fifth to the tenth century CE Britain's language was the tongue we now refer to as *Old English*. During the next four centuries the many French attempts at English conquest introduced many French words to English.

The Norman Conquest that brought the English speakers in the British Isles under the rule of French speakers impacted the language, but it is significant that English speakers did not adopt the language of the ruling class—they did not become French speakers. Even so, many vocabulary items entered the language in that period; however, the grammar and syntax of the language remained Germanic.

Middle English, the best example of which is the writings of Geoffrey Chaucer, dates loosely from 1066 to 1509 CE. William Caxton brought the printing press to England in 1474, which increased literacy. Old English words required numerous inflections to indicate noun cases and plurals as well as verb conjugations. Middle English continued to use many inflections and pronunciations that treated these inflections as separately pronounced syllables. English in 1300 would have been written "Olde Anglishe" with the *es* at the ends of the words pronounced as our short *a* vowel. Even adjectives had plural inflections: "long dai" became "longe daies," pronounced "long-a day-as." Spelling was phonetic; thus, every vowel had multiple pronunciations, a fact that continues to affect the language.

Modern English dates from the introduction of The Great Vowels Shift because this created guidelines for spelling and pronunciation. The Great Vowel Shift that occurred between the fourteenth and sixteenth centuries is somewhat of a mystery, although it is generally attributed to the migration to Southeast England following the Black Plague. The Great Vowel Shift largely accounts for the discrepancy between orthography and speech—the difficult spelling system in modern English.

Before the printing press, books were copied laboriously by hand and the language was subject to the individual interpretations of the scribes. Printers and subsequently lexicographers like Samuel Johnson and America's Noah Webster influenced the guidelines. As reading matter was mass produced, the reading public was forced to adopt the speech and writing habits developed by those who wrote and printed books.

Despite many students' insistence to the contrary, Shakespeare's writings are in Modern English. It is important to stress to students that language, like customs, morals, and other social factors, is constantly subject to change. Immigration, inventions, and cataclysmic events change language as much as any other facet of life. The domination of one race or nation over others can change a language significantly. Beginning with the colonization of the New World, English and Spanish became dominant languages in the western hemisphere. American English today is somewhat different in pronunciation and vocabulary from British English. The British call a truck a "lorry"; a baby carriage a "pram," short for "perambulator"; and an elevator a "lift." There are very few syntactical differences, however, and even the tonal qualities that were once so clearly different are converging.

Colonization of other countries has also brought new vocabulary items into the language. Indian English has its own easily recognizable attributes, as do Australian and North American English, and cultural interactions among these regions have added to items in the usages of each other and in the language at large. The fact that English is the most widely spoken and understood language in the world in the twenty-first century implies that it is constantly being changed by globalization.

Other influences, of course, also impact language. The introduction of television and its domination by the United States has had great influence on the English that is spoken and understood all over the world. The same is true of the computerizing of the world (Tom Friedman called it "flattening" in his book *The World is Flat: A Brief History of the Twenty-first Century*). New terms have been added, old terms have new meanings ("mouse," for instance), and nouns have been verbalized.

Though Modern English is less complex than Middle English, having lost many unnecessary inflections, it is still considered difficult to learn because of its many exceptions to the rules. It has, however, become the world's dominant language as a result of the great political, military, and social power of England from the fifteenth to the nineteenth century and of America in the twentieth century.

Modern inventions—the telephone, phonograph, radio, television, and motion pictures—have especially affected English pronunciation. Regional dialects, once a hindrance to clear understanding, have fewer distinct characteristics. The speakers from different parts of the United States can be identified by their accents, but as educators and media personalities stress uniform pronunciations and proper grammar, the differences are diminishing.

It is important for students to understand that language is in constant flux. Language changes in all its manifestations. At the phonetic level, the sounds of a language will change, as will its orthography. The vocabulary level will probably manifest the greatest changes. Changes in syntax are slower and less likely to occur. For example, English has changed in response to the influences of many other languages and cultures as well as internal cultural changes, such as the development of the railroad and the computer; however, its syntax still relies on word order. It has not shifted to an inflected system even though many of the cultures that have impacted it, such as Spanish do have an inflected language.

Emphasis should be placed on learning and using language for specific purposes and audiences. Negative criticism of a student's errors in word choice or sentence structures will inhibit creativity. Positive criticism that suggests ways to enhance communication skills will encourage exploration.

ORIGINS OF ENGLISH WORDS

Just as countries and families have histories, so do words. Knowing and understanding the origin of a word, where it has been used through the years, and the history of its meaning as it has changed is an important component of the writing and language teacher's toolkit. Never in the history of the English language have the forms and meanings of words changed so rapidly. When America was settled originally, immigration from many countries made it a "melting pot."

Immigration to America accelerated rapidly within the first hundred years after the country was founded, resulting in pockets of language throughout the country. When trains began to make transportation available and affordable, individuals from those various pockets came in contact with each other, shared vocabularies, and attempted to converse. From that time forward, every generation brought the introduction of a technology that made language interchange not only more possible but also more important.

Radio began the trend to standardize dialects. A Bostonian might not be understood by a native of Louisiana, who might not be interested in turning the dial to hear the news, a drama, or the advertisements of the vendors that had a vested interest in being heard and understood. Soap and soup producers knew a goldmine when they saw it and created a market for radio announcers and actors who spoke without a pronounced dialect. As a result, listeners began to hear the English language in a dialect very different from the one they spoke, and as it settled into their thinking processes, it eventually made its way to their tongues. Therefore spoken English began to lose some of its local peculiarities. It has been a slow process, but most Americans can easily understand other Americans, no matter where they come from. They can even converse with a native of Great Britain with little difficulty. The introduction of television carried the evolution further, as did the explosion of electronic communicating devices over the past fifty years.

An excellent example of the changes that have occurred in English is a comparison of Shakespeare's original works with modern translations. Without help, twenty-first-century Americans are unable to read the *Folio*. On the other hand, teachers must constantly be mindful of the vocabularies and etymologies of their students, who are on the receiving end of the escalation brought about by technology and increased global influence and contact.

In the past, the Oxford English Dictionary has been the most reliable source for etymologies. Some of the collegiate dictionaries are also useful. *Merriam-Webster's 3rd Unabridged Dictionary* is useful in tracing the sources of words in American English. *Merriam-Webster's Unabridged Dictionary* may be out of date, so a teacher should also have a *Merriam-Webster's Collegiate Dictionary*, which is updated regularly.

However, there are many up-to-date sources for keeping up with and keeping track of the changes that have occurred and are occurring constantly. Google "etymology," for instance, or a word meaning can be found in a multitude of sources. However, don't trust a single source. The information should be validated by at least three sources. Wikipedia is very useful, but it can be changed by anyone who chooses, so any information on it should be backed up by other sources.

In order to know when to label a usage "jargon" or "colloquial," the teacher must be aware of the possibility that a word once deemed jargon is now accepted as standard. In order to remain current, the teacher must continually keep up with the etymological aids that are available, particularly online.

SPELLING HISTORY

Spelling in English is complicated by the fact that it is not phonetic—that is, it is not based on the one-sound/one letter formula used by many other languages. The reason for this is that it is based on the Latin alphabet, which originally had twenty letters, consisting of the present English alphabet minus J, K, V, W, Y, and Z. The Romans added K to be used in abbreviations and Y and Z in words that came from the Greek. This 23-letter alphabet was adopted by the English, who developed W as a ligatured doubling of U and later developed J and V as consonantal variants of I and U. The result was our alphabet of 26 letters with uppercase (capital) and lowercase forms.

Spelling is based primarily on fifteenth-century English. The problem is that pronunciation has changed drastically since then, especially long vowels and diphthongs. This Great Vowel Shift affected the seven long vowels. For a long time, spelling was erratic—there were no standards. As long as the meaning was clear, spelling was not considered very important. Samuel Johnson tackled this problem, and his *Dictionary of the English Language* (1755) brought standards to spelling, which were important once printing presses were invented. There have been some changes through the years but spelling is still not strictly phonetic. There have been many attempts to nudge the spelling into a more phonetic representation of the sounds, but for the most part they have failed. A good example is Noah Webster's *Spelling Book* (1783), which was a precursor to the first edition (1828) of his *American Dictionary of the English Language*.

While there are rules for spelling, and it's important that students learn the rules, there are many exceptions, and memorizing exceptions and giving plenty of opportunities for practicing them seems the only solution for the teacher of English.

COMPETENCY 3.0 Composition and Rhetoric

Skill 3.1 Understanding strategies for teaching writing and theories of how students learn to write

The following process will help you prepare for the essay portion of your test. It will also help students prepare for writing an essay.

Prior to writing, prewrite for ideas and details as well as to decide how your essay will be organized. In the one-hour timed writing, you should spend no more than 5 to 10 minutes prewriting and organizing your ideas. As you prewrite, it might be helpful to remember you should have at least three main points and at least two to three details to support each of your main ideas. There are several types of graphic organizers that you should practice using as you prepare for the essay portion of the test.

PREWRITE TO EXPLAIN HOW OR WHY

Select a poem and, using the visual organizer on the following page, explain how a poet creates tone and mood through imagery and word choice. For a poem, you may want to start at the bottom of the organizer and work up. Begin by identifying the imagery and diction. Notice patterns and place the examples from the poem in the boxes by type, such as visual imagery, figurative language, alliteration, angry words, sound words, etc. In each reason box, include these types. Any pattern should help reveal the mood and the tone of the poem. Place the mood and the tone in the main idea box. Depending on the poem, you may need additional boxes. Also remember that the *mood* is the feeling in the poem. The *tone* is the attitude of the speaker towards her subject. Mood and tone are not always the same. Identifying the tone will help you understand the poem's theme.

VISUAL ORGANIZER: GIVING REASONS

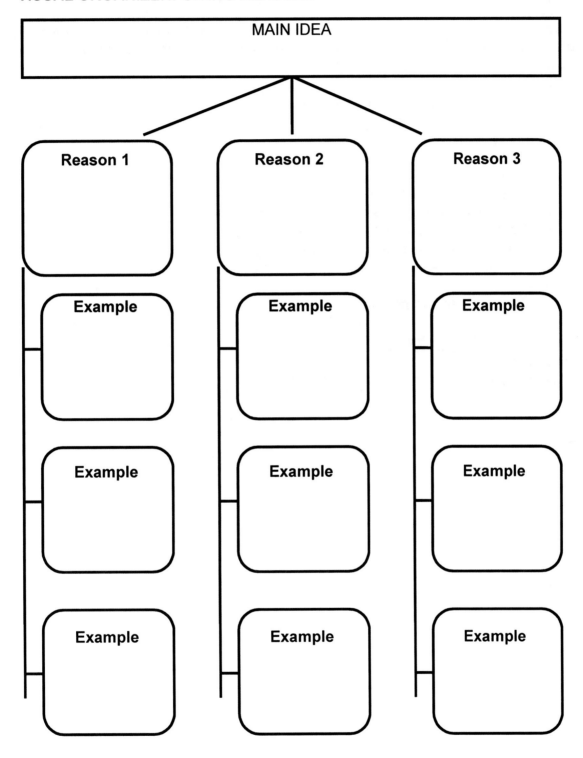

PREWRITE TO ORGANIZE IDEAS

After you have completed a graphic organizer you need to decide how you will organize your essay. To organize your essay, you might consider one of the following patterns.

1. Examine individual elements such as **plot**, **setting**, **theme**, **character**, **point of view**, **tone**, **mood**, or **style**.

SINGLE ELEMENT OUTLINE

- ⊙ Intro: Main idea statement
- ⊙ Main point 1 with at least two supporting details
- ⊙ Main point 2 with at least two supporting details
- ⊙ Main point 3 with at least two supporting details
- ⊙ Conclusion (restates main ideas and summary of main points)

2. Compare and contrast two elements.

POINT-BY-POINT	BLOCK
Introduction Statement of main idea about A and B	Introduction Statement of main idea about A and B
Main Point 1 Discussion of A Discussion of B	Discussion of A Main Point 1 Main Point 2 Main Point 3
Main Point 2 Discussion of A Discussion of B	Discussion of B Main Point 1 Main Point 2 Main Point 3
Main Point 3 Discussion of A Discussion of B	Conclusion Restatement of main idea
Conclusion Restatement or summary of main idea	

Practice

Using the cluster on the next page, prewrite ideas for analyzing another poem or identifying how the author develops a character or theme in a novel. (When creating a prewriting graphic organizer for students, match the organizer with the task.)

VISUAL ORGANIZER: GIVING INFORMATION

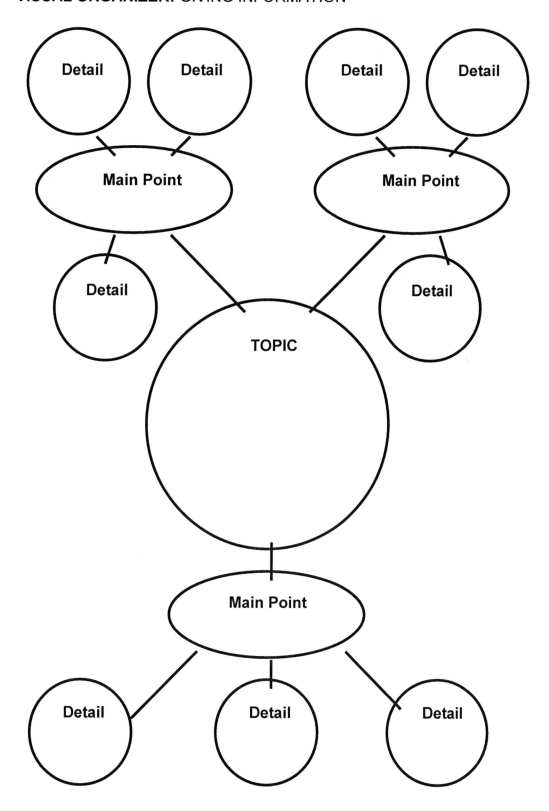

Seeing writing as a process is very helpful in saving preparation time, particularly in the taking of notes and the development of drafts. When writing for a test, the audience and purpose are clearly stated. Be sure to write with an academic tone and pay attention to correct mechanics and usage.

STUDENTS AND THE WRITING PROCESS

Expository and Persuasive Essay

When teaching students to write an expository or persuasive essay, audience and purpose must be determined. A preliminary review of literature is helpful. For example, if the topic is immigration, a cursory review of the various points of view in the debate going on in the country will help the writer decide what this particular written piece will try to accomplish. The purpose could be to review the various points of view, which would be an informative purpose. On the other hand, the writer might want to take a point of view and provide proof and support with the purpose of changing the reader's mind. The writer might even want the reader to take some action as a result of reading. Another possible purpose might be simply to write a description of a family of immigrants.

Once a cursory review has been completed, it is time to begin research in earnest and to prepare to take notes. If the thesis has been clearly defined and some thought has been given to what will be used to prove or support this thesis, a tentative outline can be developed. A thesis plus three points is typical. However, less importance is now given to this "formulaic" five-paragraph structure in an essay. Instead, writing that is organized and possesses a strong voice is what really matters.

Decisions about introduction and conclusion should be deferred until the body of the paper is written. Note-taking is much more effective if the notes are being taken to provide information for an outline. With this purpose in mind it is less likely that the writer will go off on time-consuming tangents when taking notes.

Formal outlines inhibit effective writing. However, a loosely constructed outline can be an effective device for note-taking that will yield the information for a worthwhile statement about a topic. Sentence outlines are better than topic outlines because they require the writer to do some thinking about the direction a subtopic will take.

Once this preliminary note-taking phase is over, the first draft can be developed. The writing at this stage is likely to be highly individualistic. However, successful writers tend to just write, keeping in mind the purpose of the paper, the point that is going to be made, and the information that has been turned up in the research. Student writers need to understand that this first draft is just that—the first one. It takes more than one draft to write a worthwhile statement about a topic. This is what successful writers do. It can be helpful to have students read the various drafts of a story by a well-known writer.

Once the draft is on paper, a stage that is sometimes called **revision** occurs. Revision is rereading objectively, testing the effectiveness on a reader of the arrangement and the line of reasoning. The kinds of changes that will need to be made are rearranging the parts, changing words, adding information that is missing but necessary, and deleting information that doesn't fit or contribute to the accomplishment of the purpose.

Once the body of the paper has been shaped to the writer's satisfaction, the introduction and conclusion should be fashioned. An introduction should grab the reader's interest and perhaps announce the purpose and thesis of the paper unless the reasoning is inductive. In this case purpose and thesis may come later in the paper. The conclusion must reaffirm the purpose in some way.

Finally, the paper should be edited for correct grammar and mechanics.

Tips for Revising an Essay

Enhancing interest:

- ⊙ Start out with an attention-grabbing introduction. This sets an engaging tone for the entire piece and will be more likely to engage the reader.
- ⊙ Use dynamic vocabulary and varied sentence beginnings and sentence structures. Keep the readers on their toes. If they can predict what you are going to say next, switch it up.
- ⊙ Avoid using clichés (as cold as ice, the best thing since sliced bread, nip it in the bud). These are easy shortcuts but they are not interesting, memorable, or convincing.

Ensuring understanding:

- ⊙ Avoid using words like "clearly," "obviously," and "undoubtedly." Often things that are clear or obvious to the author are not as apparent to the reader. Instead of using these words, make your point so strongly that it is clear on its own.
- ⊙ Use the word that best fits the meaning you intend, even if it is longer or a little less common. Try to find a balance and choose a familiar yet precise word.
- ⊙ When in doubt, explain further.

Techniques to maintain focus:

- ⊙ **Focus on a main point.** The point should be clear to readers and all sentences in the paragraph should relate to it.

- ⊙ **Start the paragraph with a topic sentence.** This should be a general, one-sentence summary of the paragraph's main point, relating both back toward the thesis and toward the content of the paragraph. A topic sentence is sometimes unnecessary if the paragraph continues a developing idea clearly introduced in a preceding paragraph or if the paragraph appears in a narrative of events where generalizations might interrupt the flow of the story.
- ⊙ **Stick to the point.** Eliminate sentences that do not support the topic sentence.
- ⊙ **Be flexible.** If there is not enough evidence to support the claim your topic sentence is making do not fall into the trap of wandering or introducing new ideas within the paragraph. Either find more evidence or adjust the topic sentence to collaborate with the evidence that is available.

Narrative Writing

It seems simplistic, yet it's true: The first and most important measure of a story is the story itself. *The story's the thing*. However, a good story must have certain elements and characteristics.

Plot is the series of events, involving conflict, that make up the story. Without conflict there is no story, so determining what the conflicts are should be a priority for the writer. Once the conflicts are determined, the outcome of the story must be decided. Who wins? Who loses? What factors go into making one side of the equation win out over the other? The pattern of the plot is also an important consideration. Where is the climax going to occur? Is denouement necessary? Does the reader need to see the unwinding of all the strands? Many stories fail because a denouement is needed but not supplied.

Characterization, the choice the writer makes about the devices he or she will use to reveal character, requires an understanding of human nature and the artistic skill to convey a personality to the reader. This is usually accomplished subtly through dialogue, interior monologue, description, and the character's actions and behavior. In some successful stories, the writer comes right out and tells the reader what this character is like. However, sometimes there will be discrepancies between what the narrator tells the reader about the character and what is revealed about the character, in which case the narrator is unreliable, and that unreliability of the voice on which the reader must depend becomes an important and significant device for understanding the story. (See also Skill 1.2 Characterization)

Point of view is essentially the eyes through which the reader sees the action. It is a powerful tool not only for the writer but also for the enjoyment and understanding of the reader. The writer must choose among several possibilities: first-person narrator objective, first-person narrator omniscient, third-person objective, third-person omniscient, and third-person limited omniscient.

The most common point of view is the third-person objective. If the story is seen from this point of view, the reader watches the action, hears the dialogue, and reads descriptions and must deduce characterization from all of these. In third-person objective, an unseen narrator tells the reader what is happening, using the third-person pronouns: *he, she, it, they*. The effect of this point of view is usually a feeling of distance from the plot.

More responsibility is on the reader to make judgments than in other points of view. However, the author may intrude and evaluate or comment on the characters or the action.

The first-person narrator is also a common point of view. The reader sees the action through the eyes of a character in the story who is also telling the story. In writing about a story that uses this voice, the writer must analyze the narrator as a character. What sort of person is he or she? What is this character's position in the story—observer, commentator, or actor? Can the narrator be believed, or is he or she biased? The value of this voice is that, while the reader is able to follow the narrator around and see what is happening through that character's eyes, the reader is also able to feel what the narrator feels. For this reason the writer can involve the reader more intensely in the story itself and move the reader by invoking feelings—pity, sorrow, anger, hate, confusion, disgust, etc. Many of the most memorable novels are written in this point of view.

Another narrative voice often used may best be titled "omniscient" because the reader is able to get into the mind of more than one character or sometimes all the characters. This point of view can also bring greater involvement of the reader in the story. By knowing what a character is thinking and feeling the reader is able to empathize when a character feels great pain and sorrow, which tends to make a work memorable. On the other hand, knowing what a character is thinking makes it possible to get into the mind of a pathological murderer and may elicit horror or disgust.

Style, the unique way a writer uses language, is often the writer's signature. The reader does not need to be told that William Faulkner wrote a story to know this because his style is so distinctive that his work is immediately recognizable.

The writer must be cognizant of his or her own strengths and weaknesses and continually work to hone the way sentences are written, words are chosen, and descriptions are crafted until they are razor sharp. The best advice to the aspiring writer is to read the works of successful writers. If a writer wants to write a best-seller, then the writer needs to be reading best-sellers.

Writing Poetry

Writing poetry in the twenty-first century is quite different from writing poetry in earlier periods. There was a time when a poem was required to fit a certain pattern or scheme. Poetry was once defined as a piece of writing made up of end-rhymes. No more. The rhymed poem makes up only a small percentage of worthwhile and successful poems written today.

A good poet uses strong and unique descriptions and strong imagery. Imagery is language that appeals to one or more of the five senses. A good poem makes it possible for the reader to experience an emotional event—seeing a mountain range as the sun dawns, watching small children on a playground, smelling the fragrance of a rose, hearing a carillon peal a religious tune at sunset, or feeling fine silk under one's fingers. Creating language that makes that experience available to the readers is only the first step. The ultimate goal is to evoke an emotional response; for example, feeling the horror of the battleground, weeping with the mother whose child was drowned, or exulting with a winning soccer team. It's not enough to tell the reader what an experience is like. It's the *showing* that is important.

The aspiring poet should know the possibilities as well as the limitations of this genre. A poem can tell a story, for instance, but the emotional response is more important than the story itself. Edgar Allen Poe, in an 1842 review of Hawthorne's *Twice-Told Tales* in *Graham's Magazine* had important advice for the writer of poetry: ". . . the unity of effect or impression is a point of the greatest importance." Even though he considered the tale or short story the best way to achieve this, he wrote several memorable poems and much of his prose writing is considered by most critics to be as close to poetry as it is to prose. In an 1847 expansion of his critique of Hawthorne's works, Poe also wrote, ". . .true originality . . . is that which, in bringing out the half-formed, the reluctant, or the unexpressed fancies of mankind, or in exciting the more delicate pulses of the heart's passion, or in giving birth to some universal sentiment or instinct in embryo, thus combines with the pleasurable effect of *apparent* novelty, a real egoistic delight."

Play Writing

Play writing uses many of the same skills that are necessary for successful story writing. However, in addition to those skills, there are many more required of the writer who wishes his or her story to be told on stage or on film. The point of view, of course, is always objective unless the writer uses the Shakespearean device of the soliloquy, where a player steps forward and gives information about what's going on. The audience must figure out the meaning of the play on the basis of the actions and speeches of the actors.

A successful playwright is expert in characterization as described above in the section on Narrative Writing.

Setting is an important feature of the play. Plays often have only one setting because changing settings is difficult and disrupting. This calls for a very special kind of writing. The entire action of the play must either take place within the setting or be brought forth in that setting by characters' reporting or recounting of what is going on outside the setting. The writer must determine what the setting will be. The building and creation of the set is in the hands of the stagecraft artist, one who specializes in settings.

The **plot** of most plays is rising; that is, the conflicts are introduced early in the play and continue to develop and intensify over the course of the play. As a general rule the climax is the last thing that happens before the final curtain falls. However, there are variations to this structure. Plots of plays demonstrate the same breadth of patterns that the plots of stories do. For example, a play may end with nothing resolved. Denouement is less likely to follow a climax in a play than in a story, but epilogues do sometimes occur. (See the section above for more on Plot.)

Skill 3.2 Recognizing individual and collaborative approaches to teaching writing

Viewing writing as a process allows teachers and students to see the writing classroom as a cooperative workshop where students and teachers encourage and support each other. Listed below are some techniques to help teachers facilitate and create a supportive classroom environment.

1. Create peer response/support groups that are working on similar writing assignments. The members help each other in all stages of the writing process—prewriting, writing, revising, editing, and publishing.

2. Provide several prompts to give students the freedom to write on a topic of their own. Writing should be generated from personal experience and students should be introduced to in-class journals. One effective way to get into writing is to let students write often and freely about their own lives without having to worry about grades or evaluation.

3. Respond in the form of a question whenever possible. The teacher/facilitator should respond without criticism and use positive, supportive language.

4. Respond to formal writing acknowledging the student's strengths and focusing on the composition skills demonstrated by the writing. A response should encourage the student by offering praise for what the student has done well. Give the student a focus for revision and demonstrate that the process of revision has applications in many other writing situations.

5. Provide students with reader checklists so that students can write observational critiques of others' drafts and then revise their own papers at home using the checklists as a guide.

6. Pair students so that they can give and receive responses. Pairing students keeps them aware of the role of an audience in the composing process and in evaluating stylistic effects.

7. Focus critical comments on aspects of the writing that can be observed in the writing. Comments like "I noticed you use the word 'is' frequently" will be more helpful than "Your introduction is dull" and will not demoralize the writer.

8. Provide the group with a series of questions to guide them through the group writing sessions. Try to focus on a limited number of skills to think about or revise. Don't expect students to attend to everything.

USING TECHNOLOGY IN THE WRITING CLASSROOM

Multimedia refers to a technology for presenting material in both visual and verbal forms. This format is especially conducive to the classroom since it reaches both visual and auditory learners.

The writing process has become much easier for students because of the writing tools available on the computer. Requiring extensive revisions nowadays is not unreasonable and can be an important stage in the production of papers.

Multimedia products abound for all content areas, including language arts. Knowing how to select effective teaching software is the first step in efficient multimedia education. First, decide what you need the software for (creating spreadsheets, making diagrams, creating slideshows, writing, etc.) Consult magazines such as *Popular Computing, PCWorld, MacWorld,* and *Multimedia World* to learn about the newest programs available. Go to a local computer store and ask a customer service representative to help you find the exact equipment you need. Additionally, rely on your media specialist for suggestions and help. Check reviews in magazines such as *Consumer Reports, PCWorld, Electronic Learning,* or *MultiMedia Schools* to ensure the software's quality.

Software programs useful for students and teachers:

- ⊙ Adobe PageMaker, PhotoShop, and Acrobat
- ⊙ Aldus Freehand
- ⊙ CorelDRAW!
- ⊙ DrawPerfect
- ⊙ PC Paintbrush
- ⊙ Visio

⊙ Microsoft Word
⊙ Microsoft PowerPoint
⊙ Google docs

In addition to software, hardware choices are now more abundant and accessible. Schools and students are now using the iPod Touch, the iPad, and numerous notebook devices. These tools all have applications for writing, searching, and sharing documents.

The key is for teachers to stay abreast of the current technologies and how they can best be used for teaching the language arts.

Skill 3.3   Knowledge of various tools and response strategies for assessing student writing

When assessing and responding to student writing, there are several guidelines to remember.

RESPONDING TO NON-GRADED WRITING (FORMATIVE)

1. Avoid using a red pen. Whenever possible use a #2 pencil.
2. Explain the criteria that will be used for assessment in advance and provide students with a rubric.
3. Read the writing once while asking the question, "Is the student's response appropriate for the assignment?"
4. Reread and make note at the end whether the student met the assignment's objective.
5. Responses should be non-critical and use supportive and encouraging language.
6. Resist writing on or over the student's writing.
7. Highlight the ideas you wish to emphasize, question, or verify.
8. Encourage your students to take risks.

RESPONDING TO AND EVALUATING GRADED WRITING (SUMMATIVE)

1. Ask students to submit prewriting and rough-draft materials, including all revisions, with their final draft.
2. For the first reading, use a holistic method, examining the work as a whole.
3. When reading the draft for the second time, assess it using the standards previously established.
4. Responses to the writing should be written in the margins and should use supportive language.
5. Make sure you address the process as well as the product. It is important that students value the learning process as well as the final product.

6. After scanning the piece a third time, write final comments at the end of the draft.
7. Provide students with a clear rubric.

REVISING AND EDITING

Assessing and evaluating student writing should help lead students to effectively revise and edit their own writing. Sometimes, however, students see this exercise as simply catching errors in spelling or word use. Students need to reframe their thinking about revising and editing. Some questions that need to be asked:

- ⊙ Is the reasoning coherent?
- ⊙ Is the point established?
- ⊙ Does the introduction make the reader want to read this discourse?
- ⊙ What is the thesis? Is it proven?
- ⊙ What is the purpose? Is it clear? Is it useful, valuable, and interesting?
- ⊙ Is the style of writing so wordy that it exhausts the reader and interferes with engagement?
- ⊙ Is the writing so spare that it is boring?
- ⊙ Are the sentences too uniform in structure?
- ⊙ Are there too many simple sentences?
- ⊙ Do too many of the complex sentences use the same structure?
- ⊙ Are the compounds truly compounds or are they unbalanced?
- ⊙ Are parallel structures truly parallel?
- ⊙ If there are characters, are they believable?
- ⊙ If there is dialogue, is it natural or stilted?
- ⊙ Is the title appropriate?
- ⊙ Does the writing show creativity or is it boring?
- ⊙ Is the language appropriate? Is it too formal? Too informal? If jargon is used, is it appropriate?

Studies have clearly demonstrated that this is the most fertile area in teaching writing. If students can learn to revise their own work effectively they are well on their way to becoming effective, mature writers.

Skill 3.4   Recognizing, understanding, and evaluating rhetorical features of writing and organizational strategies

Rhetoric is the art or skill of using language effectively or persuasively. Students should learn to examine text not only for meaning but also for *how* the writer effectively presents information or argument. Teachers need to teach students how to examine rhetorical features and devices in a text.

ORGANIZATIONAL STRUCTURES

Authors use a particular organization to best present their concepts. Teaching students to recognize organizational structures helps them to understand authors' literary intentions and to decide which structure to use in their own writing.

Cause and Effect: When writing about *why* things happen as well as *what* happens, authors commonly use the cause and effect structure. For example, when writing about how he became so successful a CEO might talk about the specific events leading up to his success. The events are the *causes* that lead to the *effect*, or result, of him becoming a wealthy and powerful businessman.

Compare and Contrast: When examining the merits of multiple concepts or products, compare and contrast lends itself easily to organization of ideas. For example, a person writing about foreign policy in different countries will put the policies against each other to point out differences and similarities, a structure that easily highlights the concepts the author wishes to emphasize.

Problem and Solution: This structure is used in many handbooks and manuals. Information organized around procedure-oriented tasks, such as a computer repair manual, gravitates toward a problem and solution format because it offers a clear, sequential text organization.

Transitions

To help students identify and evaluate the structure of the text teach them to examine the transitions that are used. Have them evaluate their effectiveness.

Introduction and Conclusion

In addition to the organization students should examine the introduction and the conclusion. Examine the opening by asking such questions as "How does it begin?" "How does the writer pull you in?" "Why does it begin the way it does?" Examine the closing by asking "Is the closing effective?" "What impression does it leave you with?" "Why?"

Rhetorical Devices

The following is a list of some of the many rhetorical devices of which students should be aware when analyzing a text rhetorically. Some of the literary devices also apply to expository and persuasive writing, such as alliteration, allusion, sensory images, and figurative language. The number of rhetorical devices is quite extensive. Introduce the devices best suited to the age of students you are teaching.

Anthithesis: A clear, contrasting relationship between two ideas by joining them or juxtaposing them.

> *To err is human; to forgive, divine. –Pope*

Anaphora: The repetition of the same words at the beginning of successive phrases, clauses, or sentences.

> *To think on death it is a misery, / To think on life it is a vanity; / To think on the world verily it is, / To think that here man hath no perfect bliss. –Peacham*

Chiasmus: Reverse parallelism. The second part of a grammatical construction is balanced or paralleled by the first part—in reverse order.

> *For the Lord is a Great God . . . in whose hand are the depths of the earth; the peaks of the mountains are also his. –Psalms*

Epistrophe: The repetition of the same word or words at the end of successive phrases, clauses, or sentences.

> *And all the night he did nothing but weep Philoclea, sigh Philoclea, and cry out Philoclea. –Sidney*

Litotes: An understatement by denying the opposite of the word that otherwise should be used.

> *Below-freezing temperatures are common in the winter.*
> *Below-freezing temperatures are not rare in the winter.*

Polysyndenton: The use of a conjunction between each word, phrase, or clause.

> *[He] pursues his way, / And swims, or sinks, or wades, or creeps, or flies. –Milton*

Pathos: An appeal based on emotion. Advertisements and politicians commonly base their arguments on emotion.

Logos: An appeal based on logic. A scholarly document will be based on logos.

Ethos: An appeal based on the character of the speaker or writer. An argument based on ethos depends on the reputation of the author.

COMPETENCY 4.0 LITERARY ANALYSIS

STIMULUS

The stimulus for the literary analysis question will consist of a selection of prose (fiction or nonfiction) **OR** poetry (an entire short poem or an excerpt from a longer work).

Skill 4.1   **Describe and give examples of the use of one or two specified literary element(s) present in the stimulus**

(See Skill 1.3)

Skill 4.2   **Discuss how the author's use of the literary element(s) contributes to the overall meaning and/or effectiveness of the text**

Writing about an author's use of **plot** should begin with determining what the conflicts are. In a naturalist story, the conflicts may be between the protagonist and a hostile or indifferent world. Sometimes the conflicts are between two characters, the protagonist and the antagonist; and sometimes the conflicts are internal—between two forces within an individual character that have created a dilemma. For example, a Catholic priest may be devoted and committed to his role in the Church that calls for a celibate life yet at the same time be deeply in love with a woman.

Once the conflicts have been determined, the pattern of action will hinge on the resolution—who (or what) wins and who (or what) loses. If the protagonist struggles throughout the story but emerges triumphant in the end, the pattern is said to be *rising*. On the other hand, if the story is about the downfall of the major character, the plot is said to be *falling*. If there is no winner in the end, the pattern is *flat*. This is an important point for a writer to make because it is crucial to all other aspects of an analysis of a work of fiction.

Characterization

(See Skill 1.2 and 3.1 Characterization and Skill 1.3 Character)

Setting is both time and place. When analyzing setting, discuss how setting interacts with characters or plot. Setting can be emotional—some of Truman Capote's stories are set in an atmosphere of fear and danger and the effectiveness of the stories depends on that setting. An analysis should deal with the *function* of the setting in the story. For example, if it is set in a particular period of time, such as *The Great Gatsby*, would it be a different story if it were set in a different period of time? A setting can sometimes function as a symbol, so the writer should be looking for that as a possibility.

Theme in a work of fiction is similar to a thesis in an essay. It's the *author's message* about life or human nature or the central meaning of the work. In a story, it may be spoken by one of the characters, but more often it is left to the writer to determine. This requires careful reading and should take into account the other aspects of the story before a firm decision is made with regard to the point of the story. Different analysts will come to different conclusions about what a story means. Very often the thesis of an analytical essay will be the writer's declaration of the theme according to his or her own well-reasoned opinion.

Point of view seems simple on the surface, but it rarely is in a story. In fact, Wallace Hildick wrote *Thirteen Types of Narrative* to explain point of view in literature. (See Skill 3.1 Point of View)

COMPETENCY 5.0 RHETORICAL ANALYSIS

STIMULUS

The stimulus for the rhetorical analysis question will consist of a selection of fiction or nonfiction prose.

Skill 5.1   Identify and describe and/or give examples of the use of one or more rhetorical elements in the stimulus

A logical argument consists of three stages. First, the propositions that are necessary for the argument to continue are stated. These are called the **premises** of the argument. They are the evidence or reasons for accepting the argument and its conclusions.

Premises (or assertions) are often indicated by phrases such as "because," "since," "obviously," and so on. (The phrase "obviously" is often viewed with suspicion because it can be used to intimidate others into accepting suspicious premises. If something doesn't seem obvious to you, don't be afraid to question it. You can always say, "Oh, yes, you're right, it is obvious" when you've heard the explanation.)

Next, the premises are used to derive further propositions by a process known as **inference**. In inference, the writer arrives at a proposition on the basis of one or more propositions that are already accepted. There are various forms of valid inference. The propositions determined by inference may then be used in further inference. Inference is often denoted by phrases such as "implies that" or "therefore."

Finally, we arrive at the conclusion of the argument—the proposition that is affirmed on the basis of the premises and inference. Conclusions are often indicated by phrases such as "therefore," "it follows that," "we conclude," and so on. The conclusion is often stated as the final stage of inference.

CLASSICAL ARGUMENT

In its simplest form, the classical argument has five main parts:

1. The introduction, which warms up the audience, establishes goodwill and rapport with the readers, and announces the general theme or thesis of the argument.
2. The narration, which summarizes relevant background material, provides any information the audience needs to know about the environment and circumstances that produce the argument, and sets up the stakes—what's at risk in this question.

3. The confirmation lays out, in a logical order (usually strongest to weakest or most obvious to most subtle), the claims that support the thesis, providing evidence for each claim.
4. The refutation and concession, which looks at opposing viewpoints to the writer's claims, anticipating objections from the audience and allowing as much of the opposing viewpoints as possible without weakening the thesis.
5. The summation, which provides a strong conclusion, amplifies the force of the argument, and shows the readers that this solution is the best at meeting the circumstances.

Skill 5.2   Discuss the degree to which the use of the rhetorical element(s) is effective in conveying the author's point and contributing to the overall meaning of the text

When analyzing a text rhetorically, discuss the rhetorical structure—how the argument was formed and built. Also identify the rhetorical devices the writer used to create an effective argument. (See Skill 3.4 Rhetorical Features and Rhetorical Devices)

For example, does the author appeal largely on pathos to convince his reader or make his point and lack in any logic or logos? Which sound devices does he use to give his writing flow or balance? What diction does the writer employ? Is it low, medium, or elevated? How does the diction affect the reader?

LOGICAL FALLACIES

The use of logical fallacies should be detected and scrutinized in persuasive writing. A **logical fallacy** is false logic. Logical fallacies should not be used when making a sound argument and they should be detected when reading, watching (as in an advertisement), or listening to an argument. An opinion about an issue or product should not be based on logical fallacy; rather, it should depend on sound reasoning.

A common fallacy in reasoning is the *post hoc ergo propter hoc* ("after this, therefore because of this") or the **false-cause fallacy**. This type of fallacy occurs in cause/effect reasoning, which may either go from cause to effect or from effect to cause. It happens when an inadequate cause is offered for a particular effect; when the possibility of more than one cause is ignored; and when a connection between a particular cause and a particular effect is not made.

An example of a *post hoc*:

> *Our sales shot up thirty-five percent after we ran that television campaign; therefore the campaign caused the increase in sales.*

It might have been a cause, of course, but more evidence is needed to prove it.

An example of an inadequate cause for a particular effect:

> *An Iraqi truck driver reported that Saddam Hussein had nuclear weapons; therefore, Saddam Hussein is a threat to world security.*

More causes are needed to prove the conclusion.

An example of ignoring the possibility of more than one possible cause:

> *John Brown was caught out in a thunderstorm and his clothes were wet before he was rescued; therefore, he developed influenza the next day because he got wet.*

Being chilled may have played a role in the illness, but Brown would have had to contract the influenza virus before he would come down with it whether or not he had gotten wet.

An example of failing to make a connection between a particular cause and an effect assigned to it:

> *Anna fell into a putrid pond on Saturday; on Monday she came down with polio; therefore, the polio was caused by the pond.*

This, of course, is not acceptable unless the polio virus is found in a sample of water from the pond. A connection must be proven.

Many other logical fallacies exist, including: bandwagon, red herring, straw man, post hoc, slippery slope, sweeping generalities, and hasty generalizations.

Sample Test

Essay Question

Read the passage below from *The Diary of Anne Frank* (1947), and then complete the exercise that follows.

Written on July 15, 1944, three weeks before the Frank family was arrested by the Nazis, Anne's diary entry explains her worldview and future hopes.

"It's difficult in times like these: ideals, dreams and cherished hopes rise within us, only to be crushed by grim reality. It's a wonder I haven't abandoned all my ideals, they seem so absurd and impractical. Yet I cling to them because I still believe, in spite of everything, that people are truly good at heart.

It's utterly impossible for me to build my life on a foundation of chaos, suffering and death. I see the world being slowly transformed into a wilderness, I hear the approaching thunder that, one day, will destroy us too, I feel the suffering of millions, And yet, when I look up at the sky, I somehow feel that everything will change for the better, that this cruelty too shall end, that peace and tranquility will return once more. In the meantime, I must hold on to my ideals. Perhaps the day will come when I will be able to realize them!"

Using your knowledge of literature, write a response in which you:

- ⊙ Compare and contrast Anne's ideals with her awareness of the conditions in which she lives; and
- ⊙ Discuss how the structure of Anne's writing—her sentences and paragraphs—emphasize the above contrast.

Sample Weak Response

Anne Frank's ideals in this writing make readers clear on the point that she was strongly against Hitler and the Nazis. You can tell that she knows the Nazis are very dangerous and violent people who cause "the suffering of millions." Otherwise, why would she have written this? This fact of Nazis causing the suffering of millions of people, and killing them, is a large contrast to how much she believes "that people are truly good at heart." Anne Frank is right about her ideals. And that is why her whole book is such a large contrast to the conditions in which she lived in WWII, when everything was going wrong in the world. You can also tell from this passage that she is a lot smarter than Hitler was. That is another big contrast in the book.

Anne's sentences and paragraphs emphasize the above contrast. They are not fiction; they are her own real thoughts, and these thoughts don't cause "a grim reality" of "cruelty" or the "absurd and impractical" things that she talks about as the war's fault. No, Anne's words cause us to see what is true and real in her art and in her heart. She makes us see that love is not the fiction. Hitler and the Nazis are the ones who make the fiction. We can read this in between the line, which sometimes has to be done.

Back when Anne Frank wrote her words down on paper, everything was going wrong around her but she knew what to do, and she did it. She wrote a world classic story about her life. This story is a big contrast to what the Germans were doing.

Sample Strong Response

This excerpt from *The Diary of Anne Frank* juxtaposes Anne's hopes and fears and the evil and goodness that existed during WWII. Her words reveal the inner strength of a young girl who refuses, despite the wartime violence and danger surrounding her, to let her idealism be overcome by hatred and mass killing. This idealism is reflected, in part, by her emphases on universal human hopes such as peace, tranquility, and goodwill. Reflecting on her idealism in the context of the war raging around her, she matter-of-factly writes: "my dreams, they seem so absurd and impractical."

This indicates Anne Frank's awareness of not only her own predicament but also of human miseries that extend beyond the immediate circumstances of her life. For elsewhere she writes in a similar vein, "In times like these . . . I see the world being slowly transformed into a wilderness." Despite her own suffering she can "feel the suffering of millions."

And yet, Anne Frank believes "in spite of everything, that people are truly good at heart." This statement epitomizes the stark existential contrast of her worldview with the wartime reality that ultimately claimed her life.

The statement also exemplifies how Anne's literary form—her syntax and diction—mirror thematic content and contrasts. "In spite of everything" she still believes in people. She can "hear the approaching thunder . . . yet, when [she] look[s] up at the sky, [she] somehow feel[s] that everything will change for the better." At numerous points in this diary entry first-hand knowledge of violent tragedy stands side-by-side with belief in humanity and human progress.

"I must hold on to my ideals," Anne concludes. "Perhaps the day will come when I'll be able to realize them!" In her diary, she has done so, and more.

Multiple-Choice Questions

1. Children's literature became established in the
   (Skill 1.1) (Easy)

   A. seventeenth century.
   B. eighteenth century.
   C. nineteenth century.
   D. twentieth century.

2. Which of the following would be the most significant factor in teaching Homer's *Iliad* and *Odyssey* to any particular group of students?
   (Skill 1.1) (Rigorous)

   A. Identifying a translation on the appropriate reading level
   B. Determining the students' interest level
   C. Selecting an appropriate evaluative technique
   D. Determining the scope and delivery methods of background study

3. Written on the sixth grade reading level, most of S. E. Hinton's novels (for instance, *The Outsiders*) have the greatest reader appeal with
   (Skill 1.1) (Easy)

   A. sixth graders.
   B. ninth graders.
   C. twelfth graders.
   D. adults.

4. Which of the following is the most effective strategy for motivating reluctant readers to read more?
   (Skill 1.1) (Rigorous)

   A. providing the readers with a variety of books
   B. making reading time enjoyable
   C. requiring a set amount of reading per day
   D. including reading as part of the students' grade

5. After watching a movie of a train derailment, a child exclaims, "Wow, look how many cars fell off the tracks. There's junk everywhere. The engineer must have really been asleep." Using the facts that the child is impressed by the wreckage and assigns blame to the engineer, a follower of Piaget's theories would estimate the child to be about
   (Skill 1.1) (Rigorous)

   A. ten years old.
   B. twelve years old.
   C. fourteen years old.
   D. sixteen years old.

6. *Diction* is best defined as
(Skill 1.2) (Average)

A. the specific word choices an author makes in order to create a particular mood or feeling in the reader.
B. writing that explains something thoroughly.
C. the background, or exposition, for a short story or drama.
D. word choices that help teach a truth or moral.

7. What is the best course of action when a child refuses to complete an assignment on the grounds that it is morally objectionable?
(Skill 1.2) (Rigorous)

A. Speak with the parents and explain the necessity of studying this work.
B. Encourage the child to sample some of the text before making a judgment.
C. Place the child in another teacher's class where students are studying an acceptable work.
D. Provide the student with alternative material that serves the same curricular purpose.

8. Which of the following responses to literature typically gives middle school students the most problems?
(Skill 1.2) (Average)

A. interpretive
B. evaluative
C. critical
D. emotional

9. A figure of speech in which someone absent or something inhuman is addressed as though present and able to respond describes
(Skill 1.3) (Easy)

A. personification.
B. synecdoche.
C. metonymy.
D. apostrophe.

10. The appearance of a Yankee from Connecticut in the Court of King Arthur is an example of a/an
(Skill 1.3) (Easy)

A. rhetoric.
B. parody.
C. paradox.
D. anachronism.

11. "Clean as a whistle" and "easy as falling off a log" exemplify
(Skill 1.3) (Average)

A. semantics.
B. parody.
C. irony.
D. clichés.

12. The literary device of personification is used in which example below?
(Skill 1.3) (Average)

   A. "Beg me no beggary by soul or parents, whining dog!"
   B. "Happiness sped through the halls cajoling as it went."
   C. "O wind thy horn, thou proud fellow."
   D. "And that one talent which is death to hide."

13. The substitution of "went to his rest" for "died" exemplifies a/an
(Skill 1.3) (Easy)

   A. bowdlerism.
   B. jargon.
   C. euphemism.
   D. malapropism.

14. What type of poetry is the following poem?
(Skill 1.4) (Easy)

   My name is John Welington Wells,
   I'm a dealer in magic and spells,
   In blessings and curses,
   And ever-fill'd purses,
   In prophecies, witches, and knells.

   A. sonnet
   B. haiku
   C. limerick
   D. cinquain

15. Which of the following is *not* a theme of Native American writing?
(Skill 1.5) (Average)

   A. Emphasis on the hardiness of the human body and soul
   B. The strength of multi-cultural assimilation
   C. Indignation about the genocide of native peoples
   D. Remorse for the loss of the Native American way of life

16. The principal writer of *The Declaration of Independence* was
(Skill 1.5) (Average)

   A. Patrick Henry
   B. Thomas Jefferson
   C. Ben Franklin
   D. George Washington

17. Pearl appears as an important character in
(Skill 1.5) (Average)

   A. *The Scarlet Letter*
   B. *Moby-Dick*
   C. *The House of the Seven Gables*
   D. "The Cask of Amontillado"

18. The first African American to receive the Pulitzer Prize for Poetry was
(Skill 1.5) (Average)

   A. Gwendolyn Brooks
   B. Harriet E. Wilson
   C. Richard Wright
   D. James Edwin Campbell

19. Which period was a movement that validated strong emotions as an authentic source of aesthetic experience? (Skill 1.5) (Rigorous)

   A. Romantic
   B. Elizabethan
   C. Postmodern
   D. Restoration

20. Which item below is *not* a research-based strategy that supports reading? (Skill 1.6) (Rigorous)

   A. reading more
   B. reading along with a more proficient reader
   C. reading a passage no more than twice
   D. self-monitoring progress

21. Use the table below to answer the question that follows it.

	Math Usage	General Usage
bi (two)	bilinear	bicycle
	bimodal	biplane
	binomial	bifocals
cent (100)	centimeter	century
	centigram	centigrade
	percent	centipede
circum (around)	circumference	circumnavigate
	circumradius	circumstance
	circumcenter	Circumspect

Which vocabulary strategy does the table above exemplify? (Skill 1.6) (Rigorous)

   A. Frayer method
   B. morphemic analysis
   C. semantic mapping
   D. word mapping

22. A teacher has taught his students to self-monitor their reading by locating where in the passage they are having difficulty, identifying the specific problem there, and restating the difficult sentence or passage in their own words. These strategies are examples of (Skill 1.6) (Average)

   A. graphic and semantic organizers.
   B. recognizing story structure.
   C. metacognition.
   D. summarizing.

23. **Regularly requiring students to practice reading short, instructional-level texts at least three times to a peer and to give and receive peer feedback about these readings mainly addresses which reading skill? (Skill 1.6) (Average)**

A. comprehension
B. fluency
C. evaluation
D. word-solving

24. **For students with poor vocabularies, the teacher should recommend that they first (Skill 1.6) (Rigorous)**

A. enroll in a Latin class.
B. read newspapers, magazines, and books on a regular basis.
C. write vocabulary words repetitively after looking them up in the dictionary.
D. use a thesaurus to locate and incorporate the synonyms found there into their vocabularies.

25. **Before reading a passage a teacher gives her students an anticipation guide with a list of statements related to the topic they are about to cover in the reading material. She asks the students to indicate their agreement or disagreement with each statement on the guide. This activity is intended to (Skill 1.6) (Rigorous)**

A. elicit students' prior knowledge of the topic and set a purpose for reading.
B. help students to identify the main ideas and supporting details in the text.
C. help students to synthesize information from the text.
D. help students to visualize the concepts and terms in the text.

26. **Among junior-high students of low-to-average readability levels, which would most likely stir reading interest? (Skill 1.6) (Rigorous)**

A. *Elmer Gantry*, Sinclair Lewis
B. *Smiley's People*, John LeCarre
C. *The Outsiders*, S. E. Hinton
D. *And Then There Were None*, Agatha Christie

27. **Reading assessment should take place (Skill 1.6) (Rigorous)**

    A. at the end of the semester.
    B. at the end of a unit.
    C. constantly.
    D. All of the above.

28. **Which of the following approaches is *not* useful in assessing slower or immature readers? (Skill 1.6) (Rigorous)**

    A. repeated readings
    B. echo reading
    C. wide reading
    D. Reading content that is more difficult than their skill levels in order to "stretch" their abilities

29. **A teacher should refer all of the following concerns to the appropriate expert *except* (Skill 1.6) (Rigorous)**

    A. auditory trauma.
    B. ear infection.
    C. vision problems.
    D. underdeveloped vocabulary.

30. **Middle-School students bring little, if any, initial experience in (Skill 1.6) (Rigorous)**

    A. phonics.
    B. phonemics.
    C. textbook reading assignments.
    D. stories read by the teacher.

31. **For what reason do poets often use allusions? (Skill 1.3) (Rigorous)**

    A. to conserve on words
    B. to create rhythm
    C. to create a rhyme
    D. to speak metaphorically

32. **The most significant drawback to applying learning theory research to classroom practice is that (Skill 1.6) (Rigorous)**

    A. today's students do not acquire reading skills with the same alacrity as when greater emphasis was placed on reading classical literature.
    B. development rates are complicated by geographical and cultural differences that are difficult to overcome.
    C. homogeneous grouping has contributed to faster development of some age groups.
    D. social and environmental conditions have contributed to an escalated maturity level than research done twenty or more years ago would seem to indicate.

33. The students in Mrs. Cline's seventh-grade language arts class were invited to attend a performance of *Romeo and Juliet* presented by the drama class at the high school. To best prepare, they should (Skill 1.6) (Rigorous)

A. read the play as a homework exercise.
B. read a synopsis of the plot and a biographical sketch of the author.
C. examine a few main selections from the play to become familiar with the language and style of the author.
D. read a condensed version of the story and practice attentive listening skills.

34. Which aspect of language is innate? (Skill 1.6) (Average)

A. biological capability to articulate sounds understood by other humans
B. cognitive ability to create syntactical structures
C. capacity for using semantics to convey meaning in a social environment
D. ability to vary inflections and accents

35. Which of the following reading strategies calls for higher-order cognitive skills? (Skill 1.6) (Rigorous)

A. making predictions
B. summarizing
C. skimming
D. making inferences

36. The most effective strategy for learning vocabulary is (Skill 1.6) (Rigorous)

A. memorizing lists.
B. guessing from context.
C. finding words in the dictionary.
D. researching the word's history.

37. Which of the following bits of information best describes the structure of English? (Average) (Skill 2.1) (Average)

A. syntax based on word order
B. inflected
C. Romantic
D. phonetic orthography

38. Which of the following sentences contains an error in agreement? (Skill 2.1) (Easy)

A. Jennifer is one of the women who writes for the magazine.
B. Each one of their sons plays a different sport.
C. This band has performed at the Odeum many times.
D. The data are available online at the listed website.

39. Which group of words is *not* a sentence? (Skill 2.1) (Easy)

    A. In keeping with the graduation tradition, the students, in spite of the rain, standing in the cafeteria tossing their mortarboards.
    B. Rosa Parks, who refused to give up her seat on the bus, will be forever remembered for her courage.
    C. Taking advantage of the goalie's being out of the net, we scored our last and winning goal.
    D. When it began to rain, we gathered our possessions and ran for the pavilion.

40. Identify the sentence that has an error in parallel structure. (Skill 2.1) (Easy)

    A. In order to help your favorite cause you should contribute time or money, raise awareness, and write congressmen.
    B. Many people envision scientists working alone in a laboratory and discovering scientific breakthroughs.
    C. Some students prefer watching videos to textbooks because they are used to visual presentation.
    D. Tom Hanks, who has won two Academy Awards, is celebrated as an actor, director, and producer.

41. Which of the following sentences is punctuated properly and unambiguously? (Skill 2.1) (Average)

    A. The more you eat; the more you want.
    B. The authors—John Steinbeck, Ernest Hemingway, and William Faulkner—are staples of modern writing in American literature textbooks.
    C. Handling a wild horse, takes a great deal of skill and patience.
    D. The man, who replaced our teacher, is a comedian.

42. A punctuation mark indicating omission, interrupted thought, or an incomplete statement is a/an (Skill 2.1) (Average)

    A. ellipsis.
    B. anachronism.
    C. colloquy.
    D. idiom.

43. Which of the following contains an error in possessive punctuation? (Skill 2.1) (Easy)

    A. Doris's shawl
    B. mother's-in-law frown
    C. children's lunches
    D. ambassador's briefcase

44. **Which level of meaning is the most difficult aspect of a language to master? (Skill 2.2) (Rigorous)**

    A. denotation
    B. jargon
    C. connotation
    D. slang

45. **The statement "I'll die if I don't pass this course" exemplifies a/an (Skill 2.2) (Easy)**

    A. barbarism.
    B. oxymoron.
    C. hyperbole.
    D. antithesis.

46. **Read the following passage:**

    "It would have been hard to find a passer-by more wretched in appearance. He was a man of middle height, stout and hardy, in the strength of maturity; he might have been forty-six or seven. A slouched leather cap hid half his face, bronzed by the sun and wind, and dripping with sweat."

    What is its main form of discourse? (Skill 2.2) (Easy)

    A. description
    B. narration
    C. exposition
    D. persuasion

47. **Consider the following sentence:**

    Mr. Brown is a school volunteer <u>with a reputation and twenty years service</u>.

    Which phrase below best represents the logical intent of the underlined phrase above? (Skill 2.2) (Rigorous)

    A. with a reputation for twenty years' service
    B. with a reputation for twenty year's service
    C. who has served twenty years
    D. with a service reputation of twenty years

48. **Consider the following sentence:**

    Joe <u>didn't hardly know his cousin Fred</u>, who'd had a rhinoplasty.

    Which word group below best conveys the intended meaning of the underlined section above? (Skill 2.2) (Average)

    A. hardly did know his cousin Fred
    B. didn't know his cousin Fred hardly
    C. hardly knew his cousin Fred
    D. didn't know his cousin Fred

49. The sentence "Each educator must include clear standards and learning goals as part of his or her lesson plan" is an example of (Skill 2.2) (Easy)

A. bowdlerism.
B. euphemism.
C. jargon.
D. malapropism

50. The arrangement and relationship of words in sentences or sentence structures best describes (Skill 2.2) (Average)

A. style.
B. discourse.
C. thesis.
D. syntax.

51. Which aspect of language shows the most evident change over time? (Skill 2.3) (Average)

A. phonetics
B. vocabulary
C. syntax
D. spelling

52. The Old English period refers to (Skill 2.3) (Average)

A. The fourth century CE.
B. The third through the eighth century CE.
C. The fifth through the tenth century CE.
D. The fifth through the eighth century CE.

53. What factor below introduced Modern English? (Skill 2.3) (Rigorous)

A. the Great Vowel Shift
B. the printing press
C. the invasion of the Normans
D. phonetic spelling

54. Which of the following is *not* true about English? (Skill 2.3) (Rigorous)

A. English is the easiest language to learn.
B. English is the least inflected language.
C. English has the most extensive vocabulary of any language.
D. English originated as a Germanic tongue.

55. If a student uses slang and expletives, what is the best course of action to take in order to improve the student's formal communication skills? (Skill 3.1) (Rigorous)

   A. Ask the student to rephrase his or her writing; that is, translate it into language appropriate for the school principal to read.
   B. Refuse to read the student's papers until he or she conforms to a more literate style.
   C. Ask the student to read his or her work aloud to the class for peer evaluation.
   D. Rewrite the inappropriate passages to show the student the right form of expression

56. Oral debate is most closely associated with which form of discourse? (Skill 3.1) (Average)

   A. description
   B. exposition
   C. narration
   D. persuasion

57. A composition with no voice will lack which of the following qualities? (Skill 3.1) (Rigorous)

   A. organization
   B. appeal
   C. illustrations
   D. ideas

58. A conversation between two or more people is called a/an (Skill 3.1) (Easy)

   A. parody.
   B. dialogue.
   C. monologue.
   D. analogy.

59. To explain or to inform belongs in the category of (Skill 3.1) (Average)

   A. exposition.
   B. narration.
   C. persuasion.
   D. description.

60. Varying the complexity of a graphic organizer exemplifies differentiating which aspect of a lesson? (Skill 3.1) (Rigorous)

   A. its content/topic
   B. its environment
   C. its process
   D. its product

61. Modeling is a practice that requires students to (Skill 3.1) (Average)

   A. create a style unique to their own language capabilities.
   B. emulate the writing of professionals.
   C. paraphrase passages from good literature.
   D. peer evaluate the writings of other students.

62. **In a timed essay test of an hour's duration, how many minutes should be devoted to prewriting? (Skill 3.1) (Easy)**

    A. five
    B. ten
    C. fifteen
    D. twenty

63. **A traditional student informative composition should consist of a minimum of how many paragraphs? (Skill 3.1) (Easy)**

    A. three
    B. four
    C. five
    D. six

64. **Which of the following is the least effective procedure for promoting consciousness of audience? (Skill 3.1) (Rigorous)**

    A. pairing students during the writing process
    B. reading all rough drafts before the students write the final copies
    C. having students compose stories or articles for publication in school literary magazines or newspapers
    D. asking students to write letters to friends or relatives

65. **Which of the following is *not* a technique of prewriting? (Skill 3.1) (Average)**

    A. clustering
    B. listing
    C. brainstorming
    D. proofreading

66. **Writing ideas quickly without interruption of the flow of thoughts or attention to conventions is called (Skill 3.1) (Easy)**

    A. brainstorming.
    B. mapping.
    C. listing.
    D. free writing.

67. **Computer-assisted instruction (CAI) accommodates all of the following factors in reading instruction *except* (Skill 3.2) (Average)**

    A. free-form responses to comprehension questions.
    B. increased motivation.
    C. the addition of speech with computer-presented text.
    D. the use of computers for word processing and the integration of writing instruction with reading.

68. Which of the four underlined sections of the following sentence contains an error that a word processing spellchecker probably *wouldn't* catch? (Skill 3.2) (Rigorous)

    He <u>tuc</u> the <u>hors</u> by the <u>rains</u> and pulled it back to the <u>stabel</u>.

    A. tuc
    B. hors
    C. rains
    D. stabel

69. In the hierarchy of needs for adolescents who are becoming more team-oriented in their approach to learning, which need do they exhibit most? (Skill 3.2) (Rigorous)

    A. need for competence
    B. need for love/acceptance
    C. need to know
    D. need to belong

70. Overcrowded classes prevent the individual attention needed to facilitate language development. This drawback can be best overcome by (Skill 3.2) (Rigorous)

    A. Dividing the class into independent study groups.
    B. Assigning more study time at home.
    C. Using more drill practice in class.
    D. Team teaching.

71. All of the following techniques are used to conduct ongoing informal assessment of student progress *except* (Skill 3.3) (Average)

    A. analyzing the student work product at key stages.
    B. collecting data from assessment tests.
    C. posing strategic questions.
    D. observing students as they work.

72. Which appeal is made in the following sentence? (Skill 3.4) (Rigorous)

    Without your help, millions of people will go hungry tonight and children will continue to cry themselves to sleep.

    A. ethos
    B. logos
    C. pathos
    D. Socratic

73. Effective assessment (Skill 3.3) (Rigorous)

    A. it ignores age and cultural considerations.
    B. students' weaknesses are emphasized.
    C. only reading skills count.
    D. it is integrated with instruction and is not intrusive.

74. **Reading a piece of student writing to assess the overall impression of the product is (Skill 3.3) (Easy)**

    A. holistic evaluation.
    B. portfolio assessment.
    C. analytical evaluation.
    D. using a performance system.

75. **A formative evaluation of student writing (Skill 3.3) (Easy)**

    A. requires a thorough marking of mechanical errors with a pencil or pen.
    B. makes comments on the appropriateness of the student's interpretation of the prompt and the degree to which the objective was met.
    C. requires the student to hand in all the materials produced during the process of writing.
    D. involves several careful readings of the text for content, mechanics, spelling, and usage.

76. **What type of comprehension do questions beginning with "who," "what," "where," or "how" assess? (Skill 3.4) (Average)**

    A. evaluative
    B. inferential
    C. literal
    D. narrative

77. **A paper explaining the relationship between food and weight gain contains the signal words "because," "consequently," "this is how," and "due to." These words suggest that the paper has which text structure? (Skill 3.4) (Average)**

    A. cause and effect
    B. compare and contrast
    C. descriptive
    D. sequential

78. **A paper written in first person and having characters, a setting, a plot, some dialogue, and events sequenced chronologically with some flashbacks exemplifies which genre? (Skill 3.4) (Average)**

    A. exposition
    B. narration
    C. persuasion
    D. speculation

79. **In "inverted triangle" introductory paragraphs the thesis sentence occurs (Skill 3.4) (Easy)**

    A. at the beginning of the paragraph.
    B. in the middle of the paragraph.
    C. at the end of the paragraph.
    D. in the second paragraph.

80. **Which of the following should *not* be included in the opening paragraph of an informative essay? (Skill 3.4) (Average)**

    A. thesis sentence
    B. details and examples supporting the main idea
    C. broad general introduction to the topic
    D. a style and tone that grabs the reader's attention

Answer Key

1. A		38. A
2. A		39. A
3. B		40. C
4. B		41. B
5. A		42. A
6. A		43. B
7. D		44. C
8. B		45. C
9. D		46. A
10. D		47. D
11. D		48. C
12. B		49. C
13. C		50. D
14. C		51. B
15. B		52. C
16. B		53. A
17. A		54. A
18. A		55. A
19. A		56. D
20. C		57. B
21. B		58. B
22. C		59. A
23. B		60. C
24. B		61. B
25. A		62. B
26. C		63. C
27. D		64. B
28. D		65. D
29. D		66. D
30. C		67. A
31. A		68. C
32. D		69. B
33. D		70. A
34. A		71. B
35. D		72. C
36. B		73. D
37. A		74. A
		75. B
		76. C
		77. A
		78. B
		79. C
		80. B

Rigor Table

	Easy 20%	Average Rigor 40%	Rigorous 40%
Question #	1, 3, 9, 10, 13, 14, 38, 39, 40, 43, 45, 46, 49, 58, 62, 63, 66, 74, 75, 79	6, 8, 11, 12, 15, 16, 17, 18, 21, 22, 34, 37, 41, 42, 48, 50, 51, 52, 56, 59, 61, 65, 67, 71, 76, 77, 78, 80	2, 4, 5, 7, 19, 20, 23, 24, 25, 26, 27, 28, 29, 30, 31, 32, 33, 35, 36, 44, 47, 53, 54, 55, 57, 60, 64, 68, 69, 70, 72, 73

Rationales with Sample Questions

1. **Children's literature became established in the (Skill 1.1) (Easy)**

    A. seventeenth century.
    B. eighteenth century.
    C. nineteenth century.
    D. twentieth century.

The answer is A. In the seventeenth century, Jean de la Fontaine's *Fables*, Pierre Perreault's *Tales*, Mme. d'Aulnoye's novels based on old folktales, and Mme. de Beaumont's *Beauty and the Beast* created a children's literature genre. Perreault was translated into English and a work allegedly written by Oliver Smith, *The Renowned History of Little Goody Two Shoes*, helped to establish children's literature in England as well.

2. **Which of the following would be the most significant factor in teaching Homer's *Iliad* and *Odyssey* to any particular group of students? (Skill 1.1) (Rigorous)**

    A. Identifying a translation on the appropriate reading level
    B. Determining the students' interest level
    C. Selecting an appropriate evaluative technique
    D. Determining the scope and delivery methods of background study

The answer is A. Students will appreciate these two works if the translation reflects both the vocabulary they know and their reading level. Choice B is moot because most students aren't initially interested in Homer. Choice C skips to later matters. Choice D is tempting and significant but not as crucial as having an accessible text.

3. **Written on the sixth grade reading level, most of S. E. Hinton's novels (for instance, *The Outsiders*) have the greatest reader appeal with (Skill 1.1) (Easy)**

    A. sixth graders.
    B. ninth graders.
    C. twelfth graders.
    D. adults.

The answer is B. Adolescents are concerned with their changing bodies, their relationships with each other and with adults, and their place in society. Reading *The Outsiders* helps them confront different problems that they are beginning to experience as teenagers, such as gangs and social identity. The book is universal in its appeal to adolescents.

4.   **Which of the following is the most effective strategy for motivating reluctant readers to read more? (Skill 1.1) (Rigorous)**

   A.   providing the readers with a variety of books
   B.   making reading time enjoyable
   C.   requiring a set amount of reading per day
   D.   including reading as part of the students' grade

The answer is B. The key to motivating students to read is to foster a love of reading. Making sure that reading time is an enjoyable time that students look forward to will certainly be an incentive for reluctant readers.

5.   **After watching a movie of a train derailment, a child exclaims, "Wow, look how many cars fell off the tracks. There's junk everywhere. The engineer must have really been asleep." Using the facts that the child is impressed by the wreckage and assigns blame to the engineer, a follower of Piaget's theories would estimate the child to be about (Skill 1.1) (Rigorous)**

   A.   ten years old.
   B.   twelve years old.
   C.   fourteen years old.
   D.   sixteen years old.

The answer is A. According to Piaget's theory, children seven to eleven years old begin to apply logic to concrete things and experiences. They can combine performance and reasoning to solve problems. They have internalized moral values and are willing to confront rules and adult authority.

6.   *Diction* **is best defined as (Skill 1.2) (Average)**

   A.   the specific word choices an author makes in order to create a particular mood or feeling in the reader.
   B.   writing that explains something thoroughly.
   C.   the background, or exposition, for a short story or drama.
   D.   word choices that help teach a truth or moral.

The answer is A. *Diction* refers to an author's choice of words, expressions, and style to convey his or her meaning. The other choices are only marginally related to this meaning, so the correct answer is clear.

7. **What is the best course of action when a child refuses to complete an assignment on the ground that is morally objectionable? (Skill 1.2) (Rigorous)**

    A. Speak with the parents and explain the necessity of studying this work.
    B. Encourage the child to sample some of the text before making a judgment.
    C. Place the child in another teacher's class where students are studying an acceptable work.
    D. Provide the student with alternative material that serves the same curricular purpose.

The answer is D. This approach is the most time efficient and flexible. Choice A requires conversations involving value systems that aren't going to change. Choice B risks being open to the charge of exposing children to controversial material despite parental input. Choice C is a disproportionate disruption to the student's schedule and the school routine.

8. **Which of the following responses to literature typically give middle school students the most problems? (Skill 1.2) (Average)**

    A. interpretive
    B. evaluative
    C. critical
    D. emotional

The answer is B. Middle school readers will exhibit both emotional and interpretive responses. In middle/junior high school organized study models enable students to identify main ideas and supporting details, to recognize sequential order, to distinguish fact from opinion, and to determine cause/effect relationships. Middle school students can provide reasons to support their assertions that a particular book was boring or a particular poem made them feel sad, and this provides a critical reaction on a fundamental level. Evaluative responses, however, require students to address how the piece represents its genre, how well it reflects the social and ethical mores of a given society, or how well the author has employed a fresh approach to the subject. Evaluative responses are more sophisticated than critical responses and they are appropriate for advanced high school students.

9. **A figure of speech in which someone absent or something inhuman is addressed as though present and able to respond describes (Skill 1.3) (Easy)**

   A. personification.
   B. synecdoche.
   C. metonymy
   D. apostrophe.

The answer is D. An apostrophe differs from personification in the important respect that a "someone" cannot be "personified." Also, personifications come in far more varieties than are suggested by the definition in question. A synecdoche is a figure of speech that represents some whole or group by one of its or their parts or members. Metonymy is the use of an object or idea closely identified with another object or ideas to represent the second.

10. **The appearance of a Yankee from Connecticut in the Court of King Arthur is an example of a/an (Skill 1.3) (Easy)**

    A. rhetoric.
    B. parody.
    C. paradox.
    D. anachronism.

The answer is D. Anachronism is the placing of characters, persons, events, or things into timeframes incongruent with their actual dates. Parody is poking fun at something. Paradox is a seeming contradiction.

11. **"Clean as a whistle" and "easy as falling off a log" exemplify (Skill 1.3) (Average)**

    A. semantics.
    B. parody.
    C. irony.
    D. clichés.

The answer is D. A cliché is a phrase or expression that has become dull due to overuse. Semantics is a field of language study. Parody is poking fun at something. Irony is using language to create an unexpected or opposite meaning of the literal words being used.

12. **The literary device of personification is used in which example below? (Skill 1.3) (Average)**

   A. "Beg me no beggary by soul or parents, whining dog!"
   B. "Happiness sped through the halls cajoling as it went."
   C. "O wind thy horn, thou proud fellow."
   D. "And that one talent which is death to hide."

The correct answer is B. Personification is defined as giving human characteristics to inanimate objects or concepts. It can be thought of as a subcategory of metaphor. Happiness, an abstract concept, is "speeding through the halls" and "cajoling," both of which are human behaviors, so Happiness is being described as a human being. Choice A is figurative and metaphorical, but not a personification. Choice C is, again, figurative and metaphorical, but not a personification. The speaker is perhaps telling someone that he is bragging, or "blowing his own horn." Choice D is also figurative and metaphorical, but not personification. In choice D, hiding a particular talent is being compared to risking death.

13. **The substitution of "went to his rest" for "died" exemplifies a/an (Skill 1.3) (Easy)**

   A. bowdlerism.
   B. jargon.
   C. euphemism.
   D. malapropism.

The answer is C. A euphemism alludes to a distasteful topic in a pleasant manner in order to obscure or soften the disturbing impact of the original. A bowdlerism is a prudish version of something. Jargon is language specific to some occupation or activity. A malapropism is the improper use of a word that sounds like the word that would fit the context. The result is most often ludicrous.

14. **What type of poetry is the following poem? (Skill 1.4) (Easy)**

    My name is John Welington Wells,
    I'm a dealer in magic and spells,
    In blessings and curses,
    And ever-fill'd purses,
    In prophecies, witches, and knells.

    A. sonnet
    B. haiku
    C. limerick
    D. cinquain

The correct answer is C. A limerick is a five-line humorous verse, often nonsensical, with a rhyme scheme of aabba. Lines 1, 2, and 5 usually have eight syllables each and lines 3 and 4 have five syllables. Line 5 is often some type of "zinger." A sonnet is a 14-line poem in iambic pentameter and having a definite rhyme scheme. Shakespearean and Petrarchan sonnets are the main varieties. A cinquain is a five-line poem with one word in line 1, two words in line 2, and so on through line 5.

15. **Which of the following is *not* a theme of Native American writing? (Skill 1.5) (Average)**

    A. emphasis on the hardiness of the human body and soul
    B. the strength of multi-cultural assimilation
    C. indignation about the genocide of native peoples
    D. remorse for the loss of the Native American way of life

The answer is B. Originating in a vast body of oral traditions from as early as before the fifteenth century, Native American literature themes include "nature as sacred," "the interconnectedness of life," "the hardiness of body and soul," "indignation about the destruction of the Native American way of life," and "the genocide of many tribes by the encroaching settlements of European Americans." These themes are still present in today's Native American literature, such as in the works of Duane Niatum, Gunn Allen, Louise Erdrich and N. Scott Momaday.

16. **The principal writer of *The Declaration of Independence* was (Skill 1.5) (Average)**

   A. Patrick Henry
   B. Thomas Jefferson
   C. Ben Franklin
   D. George Washington

The correct answer is B. Thomas Jefferson. Although Benjamin Franklin was responsible for editing it and making it the prime example of neoclassical writing that it is, *The Declaration of Independence* came directly from the mind and pen of Jefferson. Patrick Henry was a great orator, and his speeches played an important role in precipitating the revolution. Although George Washington's *Farewell to the Army of the Potomac* is an important piece of writing from that era, he was not the principal writer of the declaration.

17. **Pearl appears as an important character in (Skill 1.5) (Average)**

   A. *The Scarlet Letter*
   B. *Moby-Dick*
   C. *The House of the Seven Gables*
   D. "The Cask of Amontillado"

The correct answer is A. Pearl is the illegitimate daughter of Hester Prynne in Nathaniel Hawthorne's *The Scarlet Letter*. *Moby-Dick* is Herman Melville's great opus about the pursuit of a great white whale. *The House of the Seven Gables*, like *The Scarlet Letter,* is about a society that promulgates loneliness and suspicion. "The Cask of Amontillado" is one of Poe's horror stories.

18. **The first African American to receive the Pulitzer Prize for Poetry was (Skill 1.5) (Average)**

   A. Gwendolyn Brooks
   B. Harriet E. Wilson
   C. Richard Wright
   D. James Edwin Campbell

The correct answer is A. Gwendolyn Brooks was the first African American to receive the Pulitzer Prize for Poetry. Harriett E. Wilson, who died in 1900, was the first female African-American novelist. Richard Wright was a novelist and black activist. James Edwin Campbell was a nineteenth-century African American poet, editor, writer, and educator.

19. **Which period was a movement that validated strong emotions as an authentic source of aesthetic experience? (Skill 1.5) (Rigorous)**

    A. Romantic
    B. Elizabethan
    C. Postmodern
    D. Restoration

The correct answer is A. The Romantic period was a response to the Industrial Revoution. It stressed the importance of art and nature. The Elizabethan period saw art of all types flourish. Plays were written and performed for courtly entertainment. The Postmodern era was a response to the Modernism. It criticized the sharp classifications of groups and ideas. The Restoration period was dominated by Christian religious writing.

20. **Which item below is *not* a research-based strategy that supports reading? (Skill 1.6) (Rigorous)**

    A. reading more
    B. reading along with a more proficient reader
    C. reading a passage no more than twice
    D. self-monitoring progress

The correct answer is C. Actually, research shows that reading a passage several times improves fluency and, depending on the complexity of the material, also improves comprehension. The value of repeated readings is even greater with more complex material.

21. **Use the table below to answer the question that follows it.**

	Math Usage	General Usage
bi (two)	bilinear	bicycle
	bimodal	biplane
	binomial	bifocals
cent (100)	centimeter	century
	centigram	centigrade
	percent	centipede
circum (around)	circumference	circumnavigate
	circumradius	circumstance
	circumcenter	Circumspect

Which vocabulary strategy does the table above exemplify? (Skill 1.6) (Rigorous)

A. Frayer method
B. morphemic analysis
C. semantic mapping
D. word mapping

The answer is B. Morphemes are the smallest units of language that have an associated meaning. The purpose of morphemic analysis is to apply morphemic awareness to the task of learning new words. The Frayer method involves having students use their own words to define new words and to link those definitions to personal experiences. Semantic mapping incorporates graphical clues to concepts and is a subset of graphic organizers. Word mapping is another subset of graphic organizers and consists of displaying such information as the various forms a word may take as it transforms through the parts of speech.

22. **A teacher has taught his students to self-monitor their reading by locating where in the passage they are having difficulty, by identifying the specific problem there, and by restating the difficult sentence or passage in their own words. These strategies are examples of (Skill 1.6) (Average)**

   A. graphic and semantic organizers.
   B. recognizing story structure
   C. metacognition
   D. summarizing

The correct answer is C. Good readers use metacognitive strategies (various ways of thinking about thinking) to improve their reading. Before reading, they clarify their purpose for reading and preview the text. During reading, they monitor their understanding, adjusting their reading speed to fit the difficulty of the text and fixing any comprehension problems they have. After reading, they check their understanding of what they read.

23. **Regularly requiring students to practice reading short, instructional-level texts at least three times to a peer and to give and receive peer feedback about these readings mainly addresses which reading skill? (Skill 1.6) (Average)**

   A. comprehension
   B. fluency
   C. evaluation
   D. word-solving

The correct answer is B. Fluency is the ability to read text quickly with accuracy, phrasing, and expression. Fluency develops over time and requires substantial reading practice. This activity provides just this sort of practice. The peer feedback portion does address comprehension, evaluation, and some word-solving; but the main thrust is on fluency development.

24. **For students with poor vocabularies, the teacher should recommend that they first (Skill 1.6) (Rigorous)**

   A. enroll in a Latin class.
   B. read newspapers, magazines, and books on a regular basis.
   C. write vocabulary words repetitively after looking them up in the dictionary.
   D. use a thesaurus to locate and incorporate the synonyms found there into their vocabularies.

The answer is B. Regularly reading a wide variety of materials for pleasure and information is the best way to develop a stronger vocabulary. The other suggestions have limited application and do not serve to reinforce an enthusiasm for reading.

25. **Before reading a passage a teacher gives her students an anticipation guide with a list of statements related to the topic they are about to cover in the reading material. She asks the students to indicate their agreement or disagreement with each statement on the guide. This activity is intended to (Skill 1.6) (Rigorous)**

   A. elicit students' prior knowledge of the topic and set a purpose for reading.
   B. help students to identify the main ideas and supporting details in the text.
   C. help students to synthesize information from the text.
   D. help students to visualize the concepts and terms in the text.

The correct answer is A. Establishing a purpose for reading, the foundation for a reading unit or activity, is intimately connected to activating the students' prior knowledge in strategic ways. When the reason for reading is developed in the context of the students' experiences, they are far better prepared to succeed because they can make connections from a base they thoroughly understand. This influences motivation, and with proper motivation students are more enthusiastic and put forward more effort to understand the text. The other choices are only indirectly supported by this activity and are more specific in focus.

26. Among junior-high school students of low-to-average readability levels, which work would most likely stir reading interest? (Skill 1.6) (Rigorous)

   A. *Elmer Gantry*, Sinclair Lewis
   B. *Smiley's People*, John Le Carre
   C. *The Outsiders*, S.E. Hinton
   D. *And Then There Were None*, Agatha Christie.

The answer is C. The students can easily identify with the characters, the social issues, the vocabulary, and the themes in the book. The book deals with teenage concerns such as fitting in, cliques, and appearance in ways that have proven very engaging for young readers.

27. Reading assessment should take place (Skill 1.6) (Rigorous)

   A. at the end of the semester.
   B. at the end of a unit.
   C. constantly.
   D. All of the above.

The correct answer is D. End-of-unit and end-of-semester measurements yield important information regarding achievement of course objectives and the evaluation of students' growth; however, assessment should be ongoing so that the teacher can adjust instruction to meet the day-to-day needs of the students.

28. Which of the following approaches is *not* useful in assessing slower or immature readers? (Skill 1.6) (Rigorous)

    A. repeated readings
    B. echo reading
    C. wide reading
    D. reading content that is more difficult than their skill levels in order to "stretch" their abilities

The correct answer is D. Reading content for such students should be at a level where they can read and understand the word nuances, not at a level beyond such understanding and competence. Repeated readings of appropriate material build this foundation. So does echo reading, or listening to a skilled reader and then trying to imitate his or her delivery. Wide reading is an approach intended to motivate students to read for pleasure and information from a variety of sources and involves socially motivating processing routines.

29. A teacher should refer all of the following concerns to the appropriate expert *except* (Skill 1.6) (Rigorous)

    A. auditory trauma.
    B. ear infection.
    C. vision problems.
    D. underdeveloped vocabulary.

The answer is D. The teacher is the expert in vocabulary development. The other choices require a medical professional.

30. Middle-school students bring little, if any, initial experience in (Skill 1.6) (Rigorous)

    A. phonics.
    B. phonemics.
    C. textbook reading assignments.
    D. stories read by the teacher.

The correct answer is C. In middle school, probably for the first time, the student will be expected to read textbook assignments independently and come to class prepared to discuss the content. Students get phonics (the systematic study of decoding) in the early grades, and they normally get phonemics (familiarity with the syllable sounds of English) even earlier. They will have almost certainly had stories read to them by a teacher by the time they get to middle school.

31. **For what reason do poets often use allusions? (Skill 1.3) (Rigorous)**

    A. to conserve on words
    B. to create rhythm
    C. to create a rhyme
    D. to speak metaphorically

The correct answer is A. An allusion is a reference to something in history, literature, or popular culture that the reader is expected to know. By using an allusion the poet can include a reference using very few words. An allusion needs no explanation. Choices B and C refer more to the sound of the language than the content. Choice D is a figurative device.

32. **The most significant drawback to applying learning theory research to classroom practice is that (Skill 1.6) (Rigorous)**

    A. today's students do not acquire reading skills with the same alacrity as when greater emphasis was placed on reading classical literature.
    B. development rates are complicated by geographical and cultural differences that are difficult to overcome.
    C. homogeneous grouping has contributed to faster development of some age groups.
    D. social and environmental conditions have contributed to an escalated maturity level than research done twenty or more years ago would seem to indicate.

The answer is D. A mismatch exists between what interests today's students and the learning materials presented to them. Choice A is a significant problem only if the school insists on using classical literature exclusively. Choice B does describe a drawback, but students are more alike in their disengagement from anachronistic learning materials than they are different due to their culture and geographical location. Choice C describes a situation that is not widespread.

33. **The students in Mrs. Cline's seventh grade language arts class were invited to attend a performance of *Romeo and Juliet* presented by the drama class at the high school. To best prepare, they should (Skill 1.6) (Rigorous)**

    A. read the play as a homework exercise.
    B. read a synopsis of the plot and a biographical sketch of the author.
    C. examine a few main selections from the play to become familiar with the language and style of the author.
    D. read a condensed version of the story and practice attentive listening skills.

The answer is D. By reading a condensed version of the play, students will know the plot and therefore be better able to follow the play on stage. They will also practice being attentive. Choice A is far less dynamic and few will do it. Choice B is likewise dull. Choice C is not thorough enough.

34. **Which aspect of language is innate? (Skill 1.6) (Average)**

    A. biological capability to articulate sounds understood by other humans
    B. cognitive ability to create syntactical structures
    C. capacity for using semantics to convey meaning in a social environment
    D. ability to vary inflections and accents

The answer is A. The biological capability to articulate sounds understood by other humans is innate; and later children learn semantics and syntactical structures through trial and error. Linguists agree that language is first a vocal system of word symbols that enable a human to communicate his or her feelings, thoughts, and desires to other human beings.

35. **Which of the following reading strategies calls for higher-order cognitive skills? (Skill 1.6) (Rigorous)**

    A. making predictions
    B. summarizing
    C. skimming
    D. making inferences

The answer is D. Making inferences from a text involves using other reading skills such as making predictions, skimming, scanning, summarizing, and then coming to conclusions or making inferences that are not directly stated in the text.

36. **The most effective strategy for learning vocabulary is (Skill 1.6) (Rigorous)**

    A. memorizing lists.
    B. guessing from context.
    C. finding words in the dictionary.
    D. researching the word's history.

The correct answer is B. Guessing vocabulary from context is the most effective method for learning vocabulary because the learner is able to make associations with other familiar words and construct units of meaning, rather than learning isolated word that may be easily forgotten.

37. **Which of the following bits of information best describes the structure of English? (Skill 2.1) (Average)**

    A. syntax based on word order
    B. inflected
    C. Romantic
    D. phonetic orthography

The correct answer is A. The syntax of English, reflective of its Germanic origins, relies on word order rather than inflection. Because of this and the many influences of other languages (particularly with regard to vocabulary), the orthography is not phonetic, which complicates the teaching of standardized spelling.

38. **Which of the following sentences contains an error in agreement? (Skill 2.1) (Easy)**

    A. Jennifer is one of the women who writes for the magazine.
    B. Each one of their sons plays a different sport.
    C. This band has performed at the Odeum many times.
    D. The data are available online at the listed website.

The correct answer is A. "One" is the subject of the sentence; therefore, the correct verb is the singular "was." "Women" is the object of the preposition and not the subject of the sentence.

39. Which group of words is *not* a sentence? (Skill 2.1) (Easy)

   A. In keeping with the graduation tradition, the students, in spite of the rain, standing in the cafeteria tossing their mortarboards.
   B. Rosa Parks, who refused to give up her seat on the bus, will be forever remembered for her courage.
   C. Taking advantage of the goalie's being out of the net, we scored our last and winning goal.
   D. When it began to rain, we gathered our possessions and ran for the pavilion.

The correct answer is A. This is a sentence fragment because sentences require a subject and a verb and there is no verb. Changing "the students, in spite of the rain, standing" to "the students, in spite of the rain, were standing" corrects the problem.

40. Identify the sentence that has an error in parallel structure. (Skill 2.1) (Easy)

   A. In order to help your favorite cause, you should contribute time or money, raise awareness, and write congressmen.
   B. Many people envision scientists working alone in a laboratory and discovering scientific breakthroughs.
   C. Some students prefer watching videos to textbooks because they are used to visual presentation.
   D. Tom Hanks, who has won two Academy Awards, is celebrated as an actor, director, and producer.

The answer is C. Parallel structure means that certain sentence structures in key positions match up grammatically. In choice C, "watching videos" is a gerund phrase functioning as the direct object of the verb, and because the verb implies a comparison, parallel construction requires that "textbooks" (functioning as the object of a currently-missing gerund) be preceded by an appropriate gerund, which, in this case, is "reading." In order for the structure to be parallel, the sentence should read: "Some students prefer <u>watching videos</u> to <u>*reading* textbooks</u> because they are used to visual presentation." Recognizing parallel structure requires a sophisticated understanding of grammar.

41. **Which of the following sentences is punctuated properly and unambiguously? (Skill 2.1) (Average)**

    A. The more you eat; the more you want.
    B. The authors—John Steinbeck, Ernest Hemingway, and William Faulkner—are staples of modern writing in American literature textbooks.
    C. Handling a wild horse, takes a great deal of skill and patience.
    D. The man, who replaced our teacher, is a comedian.

The answer is B. Dashes should be used instead of commas when commas are used elsewhere in the sentence for amplification or explanation—here they are used within the dashes. Choice A has a semicolon where there should be a comma. Choice C has a comma that shouldn't be there at all. Choice D could be correct in a non-restrictive context, and so whether or not it is correct is ambiguous.

42. **A punctuation mark indicating omission, interrupted thought, or an incomplete statement is a/an (Skill 2.1) (Average)**

    A. ellipsis.
    B. anachronism.
    C. colloquy.
    D. idiom.

The answer is A. In an ellipsis, a word or words that would clarify the sentence's message are missing, yet it is still possible to understand them from the context. An anachronism is something out of its proper timeframe. A colloquy is a formal conversation or dialogue. An idiom is a phrase with a meaning that is not predictable from the usual meanings of it constituent parts.

43. **Which of the following contains an error in possessive punctuation? (Skill 2.1) (Easy)**

    A. Doris's shawl
    B. mother's-in-law frown
    C. children's lunches
    D. ambassador's briefcase

The answer is B. Mother-in-law is a compound common noun, so the apostrophe should come at the end of the word. The other choices are correctly punctuated.

44. **Which level of meaning is the most difficult aspect of a language to master? (Skill 2.2) (Rigorous)**

   A. denotation
   B. jargon
   C. connotation
   D. slang

The answer is C. Connotation refers to the meanings suggested by a word rather than the dictionary definition. For example, the word "slim" means thin, and it is usually used with a positive connotation to compliment of admire someone's figure. The word "skinny" also means thin, but its connotations are not as flattering as those of the word "slim." The connotative aspect of language is more difficult to master than the denotation (dictionary definition because the former requires a mastery of the social aspect of language, not just the linguistic rules.

45. **This statement "I'll die if I don't pass this course" exemplifies a/an (Skill 2.2) (Easy)**

   A. barbarism.
   B. oxymoron.
   C. hyperbole.
   D. antithesis.

The answer is C. A hyperbole is an exaggeration for the sake of emphasis. It is a figure of speech not meant to be taken literally. Barbarism is the use of incorrect or unacceptable language. An oxymoron is a term comprised of opposite or incongruous elements, such as peace fighter.

46. Read the following passage:

"It would have been hard to find a passer-by more wretched in appearance. He was a man of middle height, stout and hardy, in the strength of maturity; he might have been forty-six or seven. A slouched leather cap hid half his face, bronzed by the sun and wind, and dripping with sweat."

What is its main form of discourse? (Skill 2.2) (Easy)

A. description
B. narration
C. exposition
D. persuasion

The answer is A. The passage describes the appearance of a person in detail. Narration tells a story. Exposition explains or informs. Persuasion promotes a point of view or course of action.

47. Consider the following sentence:

Mr. Brown is a school volunteer <u>*with a reputation and twenty years service.*</u>

Which phrase below best represents the logical intent of the underlined phrase above? (Skill 2.2) (Rigorous)

A. with a reputation for twenty years' service
B. with a reputation for twenty year's service
C. who has served twenty years
D. with a service reputation of twenty years

The correct answer is D. His reputation pertains to his service performance, not its duration. Choice A implies that it was for its duration. Choice B has Choice A's problem plus an incorrectly punctuated possessive. Choice C ignores his service reputation.

48. **Consider the following sentence:**

    Joe <u>didn't hardly know his cousin Fred</u>, who'd had a rhinoplasty.

    Which word group below best conveys the intended meaning of the underlined section above? (Skill 2.2) (Average)

    A. hardly did know his cousin Fred
    B. didn't know his cousin Fred hardly
    C. hardly knew his cousin Fred
    D. didn't know his cousin Fred

The correct answer is C. It contains a correctly phrased negative expressed in the appropriate tense. Choice A has tense and awkwardness problems. Choice B has tense and double-negative problems. Choice D ignores the fact that he knew Fred a little.

49. **The sentence "Each educator must include clear standards and learning goals as part of his or her lesson plan" is an example of (Skill 2.2) (Easy)**

    A. bowdlerism.
    B. euphemism.
    C. jargon.
    D. malapropism.

The answer is C. Jargon is language specific to some occupation or activity. The sentence uses education jargon. A bowdlerism is a prudish version of something. A euphemism alludes to a distasteful topic in a pleasant manner in order to obscure or soften the disturbing impact of the original. A malapropism is the improper use of a word that sounds like the word that would fit the context. The result is most often ludicrous.

50. **The arrangement and relationship of words in sentences or sentence structures best describes (Skill 2.2) (Average)**

    A. style.
    B. discourse.
    C. thesis.
    D. syntax.

The answer is D. Syntax is the grammatical structure of sentences. Style is not limited to considerations of syntax; it also includes vocabulary, voice, genre, and other language features. Discourse refers to investigating some idea. A thesis is a statement of opinion.

51. **Which aspect of language shows the most evident change over time? (Skill 2.3) (Average)**

    A. phonetics
    B. vocabulary
    C. syntax
    D. spelling

The answer is B. History has shown that languages are more open to accepting new words than they are to making rule changes to phonetics, grammar, or spelling.

52. **The Old English period refers to (Skill 2.3) (Average)**

    A. the fourth century CE.
    B. the third through the eighth century CE.
    C. the fifth through the tenth century CE.
    D. the fifth through the eighth century CE.

The correct answer is C. The Old English period began with the settlement of the British Isles in the fifth and sixth centuries by Germanic tribes and continued until the time of Chaucer.

53. **What factor below introduced Modern English? (Skill 2.3) (Rigorous)**

    A. the Great Vowel Shift
    B. the printing press
    C. the invasion of the Normans
    D. phonetic spelling

The correct answer is A. The Great Vowel Shift created guidelines for spelling and pronunciation in the wake of the invention of the printing press. Other answer choices, though related to the question, do not answer it as specifically.

54. **Which of the following is *not* true about English? (Skill 2.3) (Rigorous)**

    A. English is the easiest language to learn.
    B. English is the least inflected language.
    C. English has the most extensive vocabulary of any language.
    D. English originated as a Germanic tongue.

The answer is A. English has its own inherent quirks, which make it difficult to learn, plus it has incorporated words, and even structures, from many disparate language groups in its lexicon and syntax. Languages with lexicons limited to words governed by a consistent set of relatively simple rules exist, so English is certainly not the easiest language to learn.

55. **If a student uses slang and expletives, what is the best course of action to take in order to improve the student's formal communication skills? (Skill 3.1) (Rigorous)**

    A. Ask the student to rephrase his or her writing; that is, translate it into language appropriate for the school principal to read.
    B. Refuse to read the student's papers until he or she conforms to a more literate style.
    C. Ask the student to read his or her work aloud to the class for peer evaluation.
    D. Rewrite the inappropriate passages to show the student the right form of expression.

The answer is A. Asking the student to write to the principal, a respected authority figure, will alert the student to the need to use formal language. Simply refusing to read the paper is not only negative but also sets up a power struggle. Asking the student to read slang and expletives aloud to the class for peer evaluation risks unproductive classroom chaos and might support the class clowns. Rewriting the inappropriate passages for the student to model formal expression does not immerse the student in the writing process.

56. **Oral debate is most closely associated with which form of discourse? (Skill 3.1) (Average)**

    A. description
    B. exposition
    C. narration
    D. persuasion

The answer is D. The purpose of a debate is to convince some audience or set of judges about something, which is much the same as persuading some audience or set of judges about something in writing.

57. **A composition with no voice will lack which of the following qualities? (Skill 3.1) (Rigorous)**

    A. organization
    B. appeal
    C. illustrations
    D. ideas

The answer is B. Voice in writing refers to an author's tone, point of view, or manner of communicating. A composition may have good ideas, organization, and illustrations or examples but without voice it will lack character and will not be appealing reading.

58. **A conversation between two or more people is called a/an (Skill 3.1) (Easy)**

    A. parody.
    B. dialogue.
    C. monologue.
    D. analogy.

The answer is B. Dialogues are the conversations virtually indispensable to dramatic work and they often appear in narrative and poetry as well. A parody is a work that adopts the subject and structure of another work in order to ridicule it. A monologue is speech delivered by a single person, most often to express the person's inner thoughts. An analogy illustrates an idea by means of a more familiar idea that is similar or parallel to it.

59. **To explain or to inform belongs in the category of (Skill 3.1) (Average)**

    A. exposition.
    B. narration.
    C. persuasion.
    D. description.

The answer is A. Exposition sets forth a systematic explanation of a subject and informs the audience about various topics. It can also introduce the characters of a story and their situations as the story begins. Narration tells a story. Persuasion seeks to influence an audience so that audience members will adopt some new point of view or take some action. Description provides sensory details and addresses spatial relationships of objects.

60. **Varying the complexity of a graphic organizer exemplifies differentiating which aspect of a lesson? (Skill 3.1) (Rigorous)**

    A. its content/topic
    B. its environment
    C. its process
    D. its product

The correct answer is C. Differentiating the process means offering a variety of learning activities or strategies to students as they manipulate the ideas embedded within the lesson concept. For example, students may use graphic organizers, maps, diagrams, or charts to display their comprehension of concepts covered. Varying the complexity of a graphic organizer can effectively accommodate differing levels of cognitive processing so that students of differing abilities are appropriately engaged. Lesson topic and content remain the same. The lesson is still taking place in the same environment, and, in most lessons, the graphic organizer is not the product of the lesson.

61. **Modeling is a practice that requires students to (Skill 3.1) (Average)**

    A. create a style unique to their own language capabilities.
    B. emulate the writing of professionals.
    C. paraphrase passages from good literature.
    D. peer evaluate the writings of other students.

The answer is B. Modeling engages students in analyzing the writing of professional writers and in imitating the syntactical, grammatical, and stylistic mastery of those writers. Choice A is an issue of voice. Choice C is a less rigorous form of the correct answer. Choice D is only very indirectly related to modeling.

62. **In a timed essay test of an hour's duration, how many minutes should be devoted to prewriting? (Skill 3.1) (Easy)**

    A. five
    B. ten
    C. fifteen
    D. twenty

The answer is B. Ten minutes of careful planning still allows sufficient time for the other stages of the writing process. Five minutes would result in more dead-ends and backtracking. Fifteen or twenty minutes would result in rushing the drafting, revising, and editing stages.

63. **A traditional student informative composition should consist of a minimum of how many paragraphs? (Skill 3.1) (Easy)**

    A. three
    B. four
    C. five
    D. six

The answer is C. This composition would consist of an introductory paragraph, three body paragraphs, and a concluding paragraph. A three- or four-paragraph composition could include all three types of paragraphs, but would not require the students to elaborate at sufficient length in the body of the paper. A six-paragraph minimum is slightly excessive, more or less by tradition.

64. **Which of the following is the least effective procedure for promoting consciousness of audience? (Skill 3.1) (Rigorous)**

   A. pairing students during the writing process
   B. reading all rough drafts before the students write the final copies
   C. having students compose stories or articles for publication in school literary magazines or newspapers
   D. asking students to write letters to friends or relatives

The answer is B. Reading all rough drafts will do the least to promote consciousness of audience. Students are very used to turning papers in to the teacher, and most don't think much about impressing the teacher. Pairing students will ensure a small, constant audience about whom they care; and having them compose stories for literary magazines will encourage them to put their best efforts forward because their work will be read by an actual audience in an impressive format. Writing letters also engages students in thinking about how best to communicate with a particular audience.

65. **Which of the following is *not* a technique of prewriting? (Skill 3.1) (Easy)**

   A. clustering
   B. listing
   C. brainstorming
   D. proofreading

The answer is D. You cannot proofread something that you have not yet written. While it is true that prewriting involves written techniques, prewriting is not concerned with punctuation, capitalization, and spelling (proofreading). Brainstorming is a general term denoting generating ideas, and clustering and listing are specific methods of brainstorming.

66. **Writing ideas quickly without interruption of the flow of thoughts or attention to conventions is called (Skill 3.1) (Average)**

   A. brainstorming.
   B. mapping.
   C. listing.
   D. free writing.

The answer is D. Free writing is a particular type of brainstorming (techniques to generate ideas). Mapping is another type of brainstorming and results in products resembling flow charts. Listing is another brainstorming technique that differs from free writing in that free writing is more open-ended and looks more like sentences.

67. **Computer-assisted instruction (CAI) accommodates all of the following factors in reading instruction *except* (Skill 3.2) (Average)**

   A. free-form responses to comprehension questions
   B. increased motivation.
   C. the addition of speech with computer-presented text.
   D. the use of computers for word processing and the integration of writing instruction with reading.

The correct answer is A. CAI does not accommodate free-form responses to comprehension questions and it relies heavily on drill-and-practice and multiple-choice formats. This is a limitation of CAI.

68. **Which of the four underlined sections of the following sentence contains an error that a word processing spellchecker probably *wouldn't* catch? (Skill 3.2) (Rigorous)**

   He <u>tuc</u> the <u>hors</u> by the <u>rains</u> and pulled it back to the <u>stabel</u>.

   A. tuc
   B. hors
   C. rains
   D. stable

The answer is C. *Rains* is a formal word that the spellchecker would have missed even though this sentence is looking for the word *reigns*.

69. **In the hierarchy of needs for adolescents who are becoming more team-oriented in their approach to learning, which need do they exhibit most? (Skill 3.2) (Rigorous)**

   A. need for competence
   B. need for love/acceptance
   C. need to know
   D. need to belong

The answer is B. Abraham Maslow's theory of Humanistic Development states that older children and adolescents exhibit most a need for love/acceptance from peers and potential romantic partners. Their need for competence is in the service of gaining the love/acceptance. Their need to know is developing, but is not their primary concern. Their need to belong does not address their emerging sexual identities.

70. **Overcrowded classes prevent the individual attention needed to facilitate language development. This drawback can be best overcome by (Skill 3.2) (Rigorous)**

    A. dividing the class into independent study groups.
    B. assigning more study time at home.
    C. using more drill practice in class.
    D. team teaching.

The answer is A. Dividing a class into small groups maximizes opportunities for engagement. Assigning more study time at home is passing the buck. Using more drill practice in class is likely to bore most students. Team teaching begs the question: If you can get another teacher, then your class should no longer be overcrowded.

71. **All of the following techniques are used to conduct ongoing informal assessment of student progress *except* (Skill 3.3) (Average)**

    A. analyzing the student work product at key stages.
    B. collecting data from assessment tests.
    C. posing strategic questions.
    D. observing students as they work.

The answer is B. The key here hinges on the adjective "informal." Assessment tests employ standardized materials and formats to monitor student progress and to report it in statistical terms. The other choices are relatively informal, teacher-specific techniques addressing more current-lesson-specific products and dynamics.

72. **Which appeal is made in the following sentence? (Skill 3.4) (Rigorous)**

    Without your help, millions of people will go hungry tonight and children will continue to cry themselves to sleep.

    A. ethos
    B. logos
    C. pathos
    D. Socratic

The correct answer is C. Pathos is emotion. Ethos is ethics, and logos is logic. Socratic is a method based on the teachings of Socrates.

73. Effective assessment (Skill 3.3) (Rigorous)

A. ignores age and cultural considerations.
B. emphasizes students' weaknesses.
C. includes only reading skills.
D. informs instruction and is not intrusive.

The correct answer is D. Effective assessment informs instruction and practice. It is one phase of an integrated instructional cycle. Choice A ignores reality and distorts rather than informs. Choice B discourages students. Choice C ignores other important ways of demonstrating growth in understanding.

74. Reading a piece of student writing to assess the overall impression of the product is (Skill 3.3) (Easy)

A. holistic evaluation.
B. portfolio assessment.
C. analytical evaluation.
D. using a performance system.

The answer is A. In holistic evaluation, the teacher reads quickly through a paper once to get a general impression and assigns a rating based on a rubric that includes the criteria for achievement in a few key dimensions of the assignment. Portfolio assessment involves tracking work over stages or over time. Analytical evaluation involves breaking down the assignment into discrete traits and determining achievement in each of those traits. A performance system refers to engaging students in writing assignments meant to generate products in a given timeframe. Often, such products are scored holistically.

75. A formative evaluation of student writing (Skill 3.3) (Easy)

A. requires a thorough marking of mechanical errors with a pencil or pen.
B. makes comments on the appropriateness of the student's interpretation of the prompt and the degree to which the objective was met.
C. requires the student to hand in all the materials produced during the process of writing.
D. involves several careful readings of the text for content, mechanics, spelling, and usage.

The answer is B. Formative evaluations should support the students' writing process through strategic feedback at key points. Teacher comments and feedback should encourage recursive revision and metacognition. Choice A applies, if anywhere, to a summative evaluation of student writing. Choice C is a neutral management strategy. A teacher can make formative evaluations without collecting all the materials. Choice D is also more suited for summative evaluation or for the very last issue in the composition process, proofreading.

76. **What type of comprehension do questions beginnings with "who," "what," "where," or "how" assess? (Skill 3.4) (Average)**

    A. evaluative
    B. inferential
    C. literal
    D. narrative

The correct answer is C. Literal questions ask for facts from the reading. The student can put his finger right on the answer and prove that he is correct. These questions are sometimes referred to as "right there" questions. Evaluative questions require a judgment of some sort. Inferential questions ask students to make an educated guess. Narrative questions involve aspects of a story beyond literal considerations.

77. **A paper explaining the relationship between food and weight gain contains the signal words "because," "consequently," "this is how," and "due to." These words suggest that the paper has which text structure? (Skill 3.4) (Average)**

    A. cause and effect
    B. compare and contrast
    C. descriptive
    D. sequential

The answer is A. These signal words connect events in a causal chain, creating an explanation of some process or event. Compare and contrast structure presents similarities and differences. Descriptive structure presents a sensory impression of something or someone. Sequential structure references what comes first, next, last, and so on.

78. **A paper written in first person and having characters, a setting, a plot, some dialogue, and events sequenced chronologically with some flashbacks exemplifies which genre? (Skill 3.4) (Average)**

    A. exposition
    B. narration
    C. persuasion
    D. speculation

The answer is B, narration.

79. In "inverted triangle" introductory paragraphs the thesis sentence occurs (Skill 3.4) (Easy)

    A. at the beginning of the paragraph.
    B. in the middle of the paragraph.
    C. at the end of the paragraph.
    D. in the second paragraph.

The answer is C. The beginning of the paragraph should establish interest, the middle of the paragraph should establish a general context, and the paragraph should end with the thesis that the rest of the paper will develop. Delaying the thesis until the second paragraph would be "outside the triangle."

80. Which of the following should not be included in the opening paragraph of an informative essay? (Skill 3.4) (Average)

    A. thesis sentence
    B. details and examples supporting the main idea
    C. a broad general introduction to the topic
    D. a style and tone that grabs the reader's attention

The answer is B. The introductory paragraph should introduce the topic, capture the reader's interest, state the thesis, and prepare the reader for the main points in the essay. Details and examples, however, belong in the second part of the essay, the body paragraphs.

Prompt A

Write an expository essay discussing effective teaching strategies for developing literature appreciation with a heterogeneous class of ninth graders. Select any appropriate piece(s) of world literature to use as examples in the discussion.

Prompt B

After reading the following passage from Aldous Huxley's *Brave New World,* discuss the types of reader responses possible with a group of eight graders.

He hated them all—all the men who came to visit Linda. One afternoon, when he had been playing with the other children - it was cold, he remembered, and there was snow on the mountains - he came back to the house and heard angry voices in the bedroom. They were women's voices, and they were words he didn't understand; but he knew they were dreadful words. Then suddenly, crash! something was upset; he heard people moving about quickly, and there was another crash and then a noise like hitting a mule, only not so bony; then Linda screamed. 'Oh, don't, don't, don't!' she said. He ran in. There were three women in dark blankets. Linda was on the bed. One of the women was holding her wrists. Another was lying across her legs, so she couldn't kick. The third was hitting her with a whip. Once, twice, three times; and each time Linda screamed.

CPSIA information can be obtained
at www.ICGtesting.com
Printed in the USA
FFOW04n1414230318
46046911-46951FF

9 781607 873457